Metal Jewelry Techniques:

Engraving, Setting, and Mounting—A Masterclass

Other Schiffer Books by the Author:
Basic Metal Jewelry Techniques: A Masterclass.
ISBN: 978-0-7643-4367-4. $24.99

Other Schiffer Books on Related Subjects:
Art Jewelry Today. Dona Z. Meilach.
ISBN: 978-0-7643-1766-8. $50.00
Art Jewelry Today 2. Jeffrey B. Snyder.
ISBN: 978-0-7643-3065-0. $50.00
Art Jewelry Today 3. Jeffrey B. Snyder.
ISBN: 978-0-7643-3883-0. $50.00
Bead Crochet Jewelry: Tools, Tips, and 15 Beautiful Projects. Linda Lehman with Shelley Grant.
ISBN: 978-0-7643-2023-1. $18.99
Beads & Agate Jewelry to Create Yourself. Connie Wagner.
ISBN: 978-0-7643-2998-2. $14.99
Beads & Strings Jewelry: A Step-by-Step Workshop. Ani Afshar.
ISBN: 978-0-7643-2731-5. $12.95
The Art of Jewelry Design: Principles of Design, Rings & Earrings. Maurice P. Galli, Dominique Rivière, & Fanfan Li.
ISBN: 978-0-8874-0562-4. $59.95

Designed by Molly Shields
Type set in Eurostile

ISBN: 978-0-7643-4532-6

Printed in China
Published by Schiffer Publishing, Ltd.
4880 Lower Valley Road
Atglen, PA 19310
Phone: (610) 593-1777;
Fax: (610) 593-2002
E-mail: Info@schifferbooks.com

For our complete selection of fine books on this and related subjects, please visit our website at www.schifferbooks.com. You may also write for a free catalog.

This book may be purchased from the publisher. Please try your bookstore first.

We are always looking for people to write books on new and related subjects. If you have an idea for a book, please contact us at proposals@schifferbooks.com

Schiffer Publishing's titles are available at special discounts for bulk purchases for sales promotions or premiums. Special editions, including personalized covers, corporate imprints, and excerpts can be created in large quantities for special needs. For more information, contact the publisher.

Técnicas Del Metal: Esmalte, cincelado, engastado y monturas written by Carles Codina was originally published by Parramón Ediciones, S.A. © Copyright ParramonPaidotribo—World Rights, Barcelona, Spain

This book was translated by Jonee Tiedemann.

Nicolás Estrada. Silver and palm nut pendant, 2009.

Contents

Introduction

Many metal working techniques are used by the crafts comprising the arts of jewelry-making and precious metals smithing. This book does not intend to cover them all. We have selected those techniques most often used in jewelry-making, with three distinct areas of concentration: paint on metal, traditional techniques, and recent new techniques.

New and surprising materials have recently been incorporated into jewelry making, many of which have improved the characteristics of the existing materials. Today, it is possible to paint on metal with the same paint used for automobile bodies, or to apply photographic images to metal by several different methods. We can utilize information technologies like prototyping and lasers, which allow all kinds of cutting, soldering, and building. We, the current globalized citizens, demand to know how to adequately combine the newest possibilities that the new technologies make available. We, global artists, also want to know how to apply new technologies with new methods of craftsmanship, which provide our work with expressive qualities and personal touches. The objective of this book is to make these applications as easy as possible, using affordable resources.

I will discuss diverse topics, among them the application of paint on metal, a traditional technique like enamel, and a recent procedure, airbrushed paint on metal. The hands-on section features an example by Nicolás Estrada where a natural material, the ivory palm, a recent addition to jewelry, is mixed with LED technology in its application as a necklace. In addition, the book shows how to cover metal with highly resistant airbrushed paint, and as the final project, a traditional mount performed with a gold piece by Joan Aviñó.

Carles Codina i Armengol

Alejandra Solar.
Alpaca brooch with images applied via image transfer.

Fired Enamel

Enamel consists of a mixture of potassium and silica, borax, and lead oxide. This colorless and transparent mixture, conveniently modified by adding diverse metal oxides and colors, provides a large variety of tones and colors. Due to its regular composition, enamel is considered a glass that, when heated to a specific temperature, melts on the metal and gives it permanent color once cooled.

Carolina Gimeno. Enameled pendant on copper, 2010.

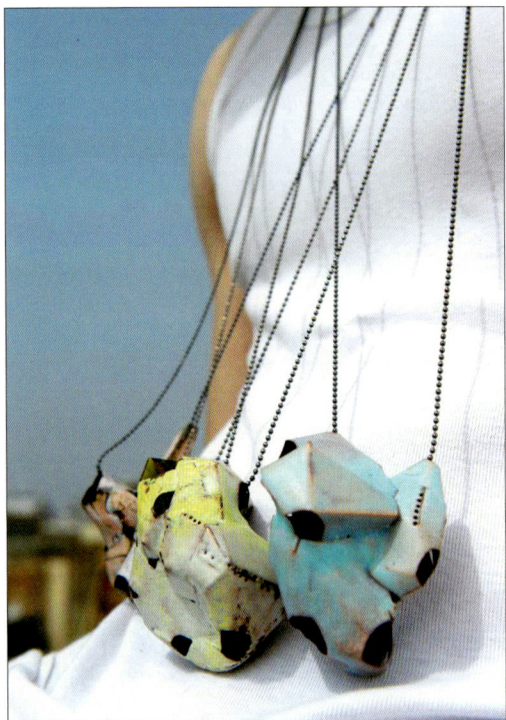

Elisabet Puig. Enamel. Printed photo on paper and wood, 2009-2010.

As a technique, the application of enamel on metal is a craft in its own right; hence, there is no intent to explain all the techniques and possibilities of fired enamel here. It is shown how to prepare enamel and how to achieve a few distinctive, personal applications. The goals are to provide colorful jewelry and to look for new artistic contexts.

Elisa Pellacani. Silver necklace molded in wax with applications of fired enamel.

Enamel Preparation

Generally, enamel is sold as a fine powder or as small pieces that need to be milled and cleaned before applying them. Once the enamel powder has been milled and dipped in acid to eliminate impurities, it must be thoroughly rinsed with water. After this process is complete, the enamel is tested, classified, and stored, always moistened in water.

Cabinet with different enamel colors appropriately classified.

1/ Pieces of colored enamel before milling and grinding them in a mortar. The first step is to break up the enamel into smaller pieces inside an iron mortar or with a large tool.

2/ Once a fine grain has been achieved, it is dry-milled in a mortar until it becomes a very fine powder.

3/ After grinding, some water is added to the mortar and milled again. Circular motions result in a fine enamel powder.

4/ Next, it is poured into a tall glass and water is added, together with two or three drops of nitric acid; stir with a glass rod and leave until the enamel, which is heavier, has settled to the bottom of the glass.

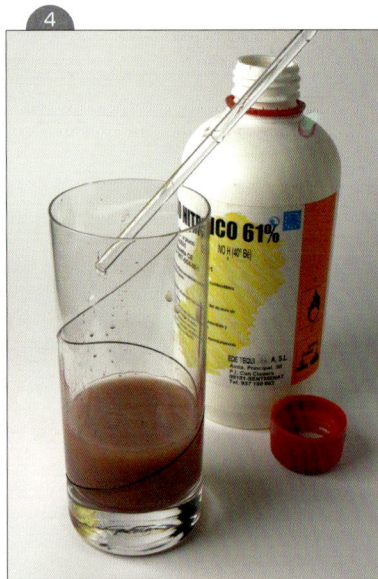

5/ More water is added, stir again, and wait until the enamel settles in the glass.

6/ Next, eliminate the water by decanting and fill again with water.

7/ Repeat this process of decanting and stirring in order to eliminate the enamel's slime.

8/ The process is repeated three to five times, until the water remains very clean. Finally, the last rinse is done with distilled water.

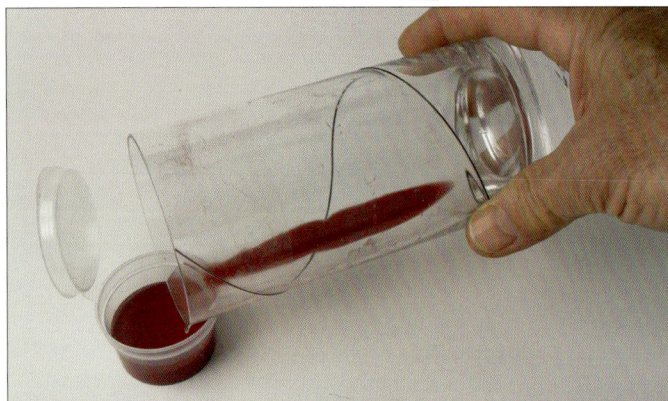

9/ Once clean, the enamel is placed into its container, where it is numbered according to its color and kept moist in distilled water, ready for its later application.

Vitreous Enamel

This is a very fine enamel applied with a brush, just like oil paint, after mixing it with paraffin. This process allows for very delicate drawings and tracings, which otherwise would be difficult or impossible to do. It can also be applied by using serigraphic cloth screens. In this case, the enamel is added with the perforated mesh of the fabric.

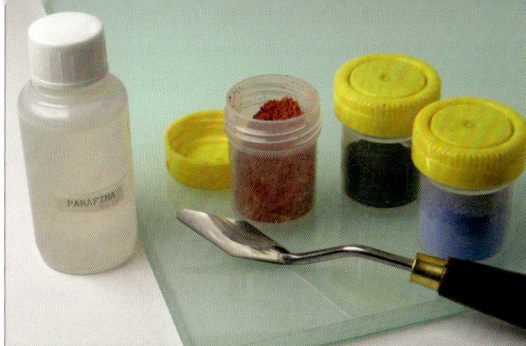

Specialty retailers offer an ample selection of colors made from fine powder, which have to be prepared before use.

Its preparation consists of mixing the enamel on top of a crystal with a little paraffin until the consistency is homogeneous. Next, store it away in a closed container until it is applied.

Carolina Gimeno. Pieces with vitreous enamel.

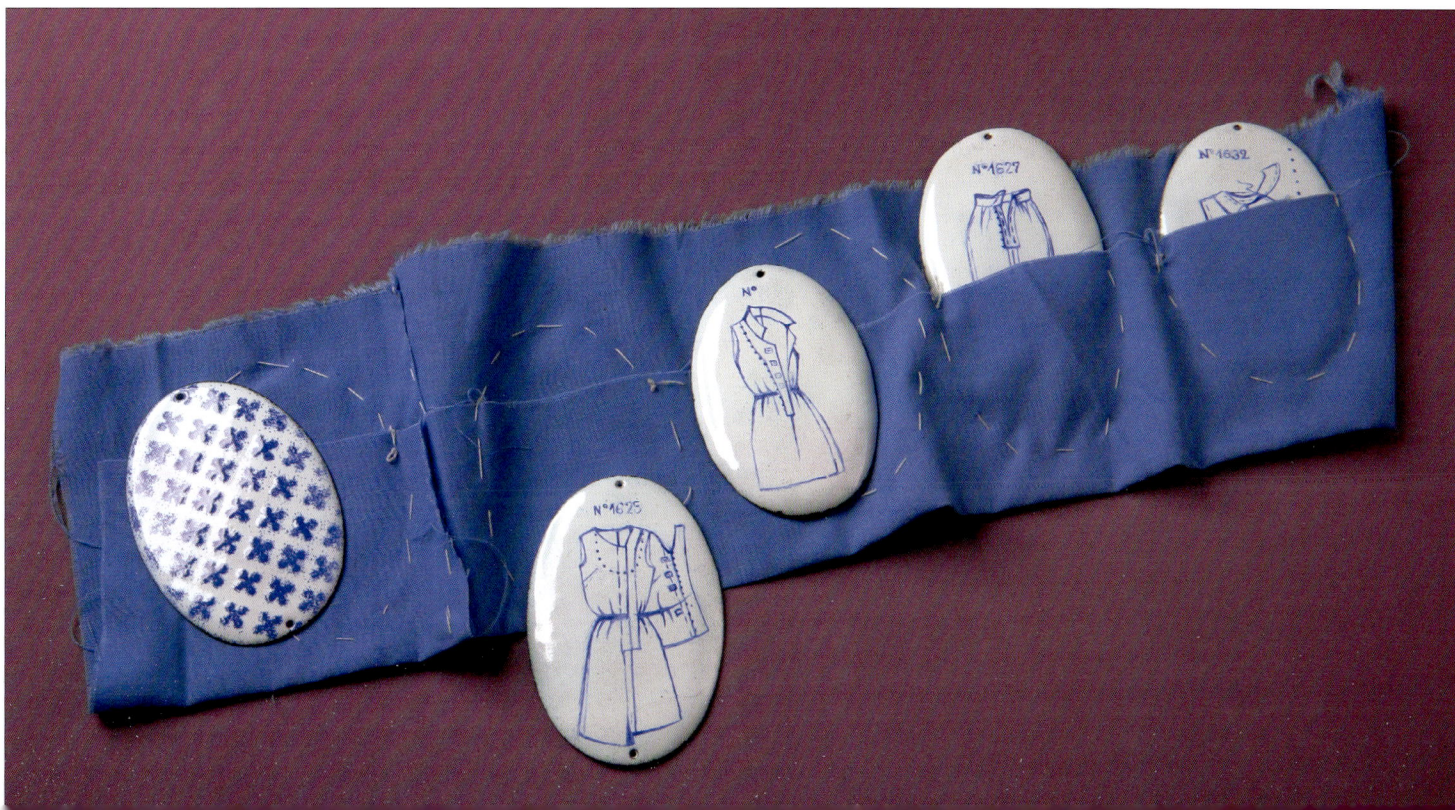

9

It is also possible to apply the enamel through a screen, like the ones used in serigraphy, obtained from a drawing.

This screen has a weaving count of 150. The more intense, the more definition the enamel application will have, as it must pass through the screen and deposit on the work piece.

Gaston Rois. Brooch made from silver with black enamel, serigraphed on a base of white enamel.

Backing Enamel

While applying enamel on plates, they contract and deform due to the different expansion coefficients between the metal and the enamel. To compensate for this, a enamel is applied to the plate's back. This is usually made by the enameler from enamel scraps, but it can also be purchased ready-made.

1/ To ensure the adhesion of the back enamel, a fine layer of tragacanth dissolved in water is applied first, with the surface being previously deoxidized and free from dust and grease.

2/ A fine layer of back enamel powder is applied onto the tragacanth so as to evenly cover the metal, then placed into the pre-heated oven at 900 degrees Celsius (1,650 degrees Fahrenheit) for firing.

The Color Palatte

Before starting a project, it is essential to know how the intervening colors will behave, as they vary according to the metal or the back enamel that may have been applied previously, as well as the number of firings that have been performed. Interesting and unorthodox effects can be achieved, like overheating and burning the enamel, which yields beautiful results.

Judy McCaig. Between. Silver, enamel, and methacrylate, 2010.

It is essential to make color palettes on different metals and to keep them for future applications.

Judy McCaig. Color tests combining various techniques.

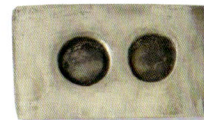

11

Application and Firing of Enamel

Enamel can be directly applied onto the surface of the object, as well as on previous enamel applications. The brush in this case is not used to paint with enamel but to evenly layer the enamel vertically on top of the metal. Once this first layer of enamel has been applied, the moisture in the mixture needs to evaporate. Place the enamel under a hot lamp or on top of an oven, which allows for the water from the application to slowly evaporate. Once it is dry, introduce the piece into the oven, which is maintained at a constant 900 degrees Celsius (1,650 degrees Fahrenheit), and only take it out again after firing. The duration of the firing varies according to the color used and the size of the enameled object. Once the surface of the enamel starts to shine, it is removed from the oven and left to cool for the next application.

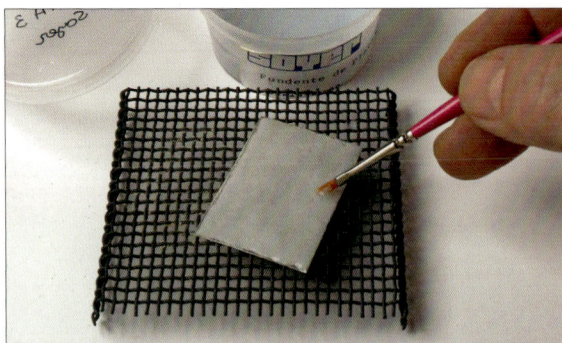

1/ **The moistened enamel is applied** onto a deoxidized, clean, and dry piece of metal. The entire surface is covered evenly using a brush, avoiding the formation of chunks and lumps of enamel.

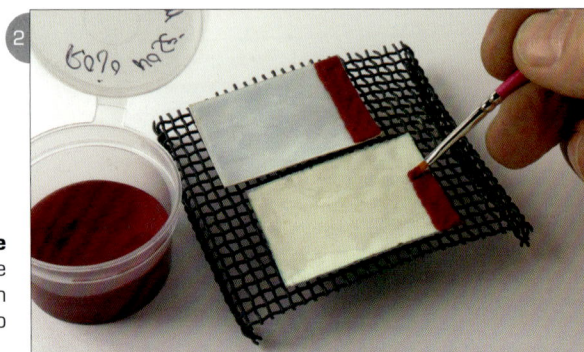

2/ **It is placed inside the oven** and, once fired, left to cool down for the next color to be applied.

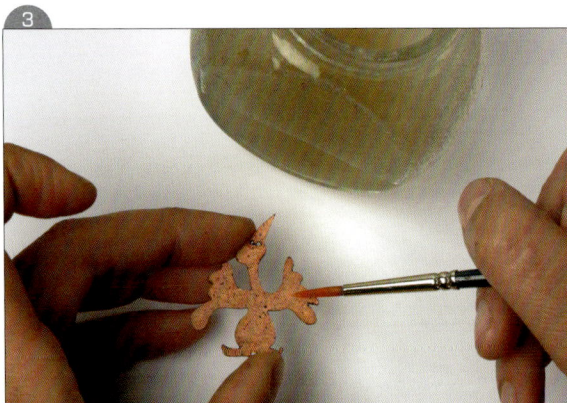

3/ **If the enamel is applied using a sieve**, first apply a layer of tragacanth dissolved in water so that the enamel will adhere to the metal surface.

4/ **A fine layer of white enamel** is spread over the surface and left to dry slowly in a warm place.

5/ Use a needle to clean holes and other areas where there is excess enamel. This avoids the holes be

6/ Once dry, the first firing of about one minute is performed.

7/ Leave the piece to cool down and apply the various colors for the particular design.

8/ Fire the piece again. Place it on a support made from refractory steel to adequately hold the piece and allow a correct firing of the enamel.

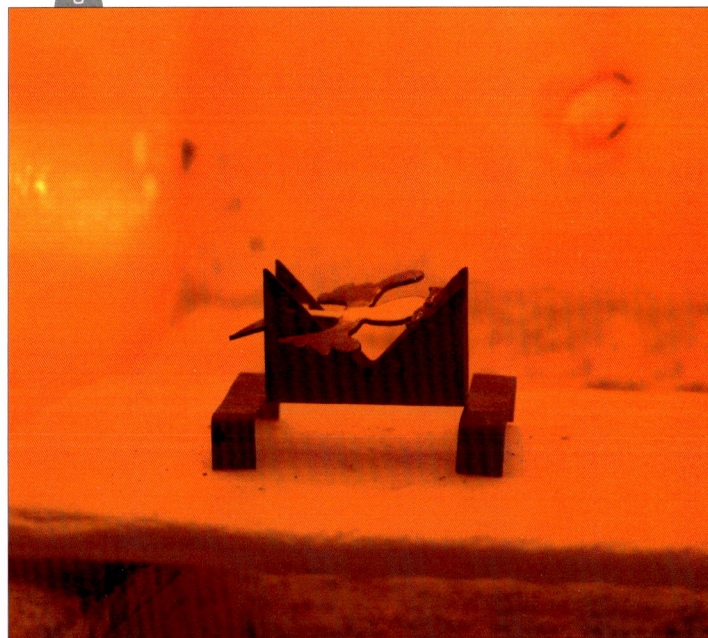

9/ Leave the piece to cool after removing it from the oven. If necessary, press down on the piece with a spatula on a firm surface to flatten the piece after firing.

10/ Here, Nelly Van Ost has applied diverse vitreous enamel lines on the surface using a brush, then the object is fired again.

Nelly van Oost. Various elements fire enameled, 2009.

Nielo or Nielloing

Without being an enamel as such, nielo has similar applications as enamel. It is a mixture of silver, copper, lead, and sulphur, which was widely used during the Middle Ages and the Renaissance. It is used to fill in the lines of an engraving, as its black color highlights the intensity of engraved lines. Currently, some artists are using it in their creations. It is an easy material to work with, requiring no oven to make it or to apply it as its melting point is very low.

Nielo Preparation

To prepare the nielo, first melt silver and copper in a large crucible, then add lead with a little borax. The last to be added is pulverized sulphur, mixing it with a wooden stick until a uniform, thick, black consistency has been achieved. Once the smoke has subsided, put the nielo onto a piece of steel sheet to cool, then hammer it with an iron hammer to break it into small pieces; next, place it inside an iron mortar and grind it until it becomes a fine

Yoko Shimizu. Necklace made with silver and gold with nielloed surfaces. Photo by Federico Cavicchioli.

powder. If the resulting material does not take on a fragile and crystallized structure, you need to melt it again and add more sulphur. The powder resulting from the grinding process is rinsed repeatedly until a fine and uniform grain of nielo has been achieved. It is advisable to sift it so that the grain is fine and regular. Once this very fine powder has been obtained, it is cleaned just like any enamel with successive rinsing, but without adding nitric acid, until its consistency is similar to that of enamel.

Silver	Copper	Lead	Sulphur
1	2	3	6
1	1	2	8
1	2	4	5

Precautions

It is necessary to use a protective mask and to work at a well-ventilated place. As nielo contains lead, it is important to avoid any contact of the nielo scraps with silver or gold while they are manipulated on a work bench. A small amount of nielo can ruin a large amount of metal if they are melted in the same crucible, causing—for example—the souring of the gold. It is advisable to file and to polish the pieces with nielo at a separate location.

Some pieces of nielo cooling, after a first grinding, before sifting and cleaning of the nielo powder.

15

Application of Nielo

Nielo can be cleaned with a little water and ammonia. Then mix it with distilled water until a uniform mass has been achieved; being a metal and heavy, it settles in deposits at the bottom of the container. It is necessary to eliminate a large part of the moisture with kitchen paper towels, and to apply a large amount onto the clean and grease-free surface of the metal.

1/ Once pulverized and clean, the nielo is mixed with distilled water. If desired, a few drops of soldering liquid (very diluted) may be added.

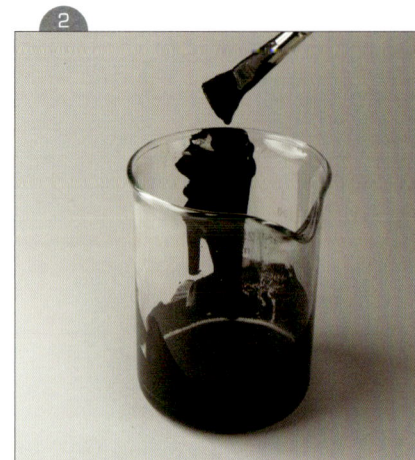

2/ The nielo is stirred vigorously until a uniform, thick mass is achieved. Set aside to allow water to evaporate somewhat, or absorb water with kitchen paper towels until the desired density is achieved.

3/ Next, store the nielo in small containers and moisten it again each time it is applied.

4/ Nielo can be applied to fill in deep engraving lines, or, as in this case, to fill in a cut made from a sheet of 0.05 mm thickness to which a thin sheet of silver has been soldered to the back section.

5/ The cells are filled with abundant moist nielo and left to dry until the moisture has completely evaporated. Otherwise, the nielo will boil while being heated and move from its location.

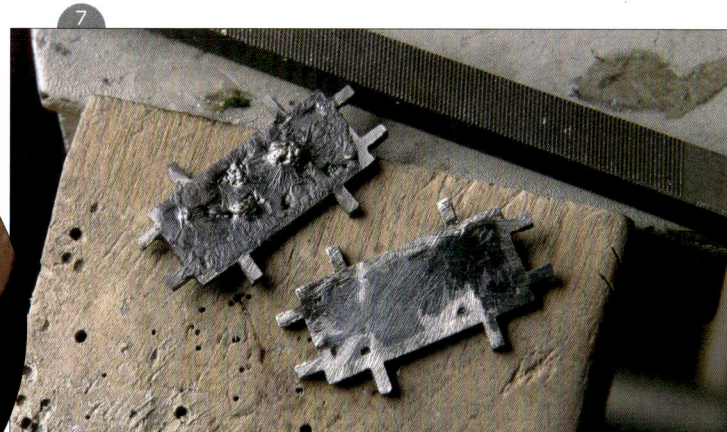

6/ Heat is applied to the back side of the piece to heat its surface and to make sure that the nielo penetrates all the cells while melting, covering them completely.

7/ Once cooled, the surface of the nielo is cut with an old file and then polished to flatten the surfaces of nielo and silver.

8/ Once the surfaces have been polished, the nielo must fill all cells completely.

Carles Codina. Silver pendant with nielo applicaton, 2010.

17

Glass Beads

Glass is found in nature, but since ancient times humans have imitated it by smelting silica with salts, solvents, and oxides at high temperatures. This is how various colors and different properties are achieved, depending on the proportions of the raw materials that make up its composition. For jewelry applications, the possibilities of glass are infinite, and making simple, basic beads only require a simple oxygen burner.

1/ Glass rods of different diameter but compatible with each other are the starting point. If glass rods of different expansion rates are melted together, the resultant glass would break when cooling down.

2/ Various glass formats, such as chips or murrine glass, can be melted inside, like those in the image, that latter of which can either be prepared in advance or purchased at a specialty retailer.

3/ The steel rods are prepared by covering them with a thermal separator before applying the melted glass.

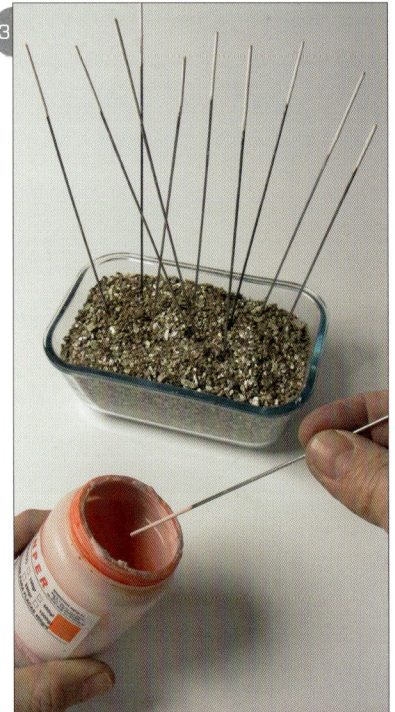

4/ It is necessary to use protective eyeglasses that neutralize UVA and infrared rays when manipulating glass, as well as a graphite fire-shovel and base.

5/ The glass rods are cut with special glass cutting pliers by lightly pressing on them.

6/ After adjusting the oxygen and gas pressure, start melting the tip of the rod while heating the steel rod impregnated with the isolating agent.

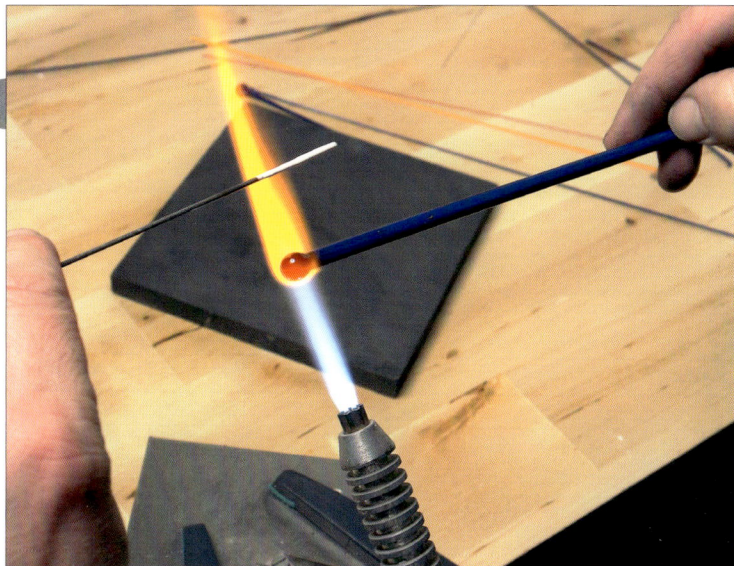

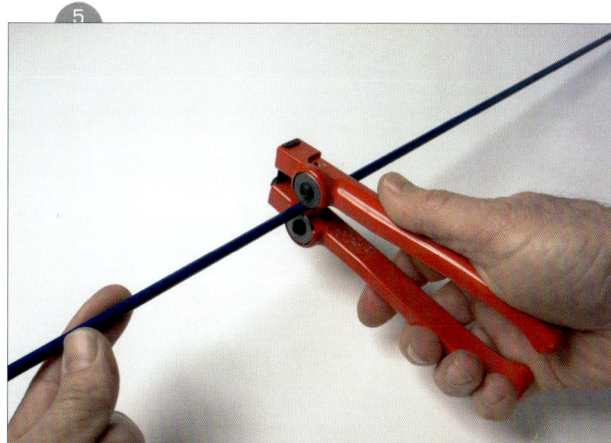

7/ Both the glass and the steel rod need to be continually rotated to make sure that heat is uniformly dissipated while the position of the support and the glass rod is inverted.

8/ Once the glass rod is heated, the molten glass is applied while the steel rod is rotated.

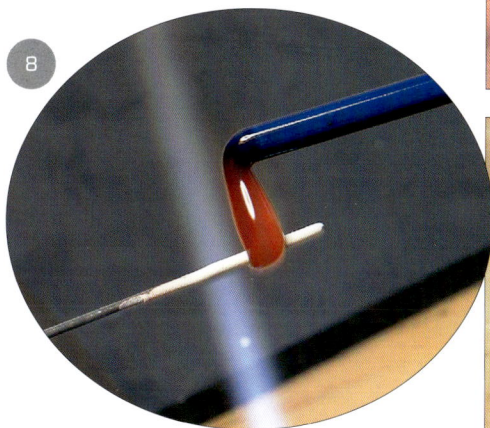

9/ Next, the flame is pointed at the rod at the right distance to allow for a uniform shape of the glass.

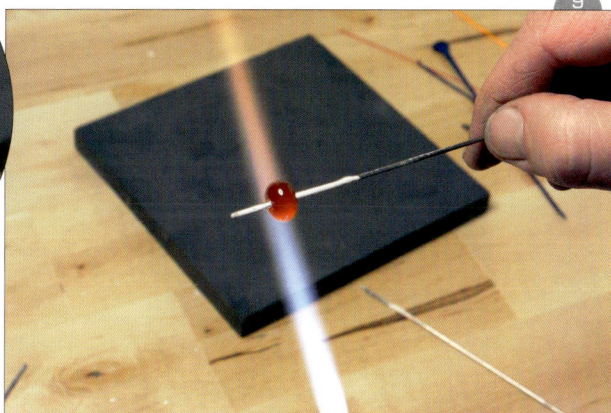

10/ New colors of glass can be applied in different kinds of layers and formats, but always while hot, to allow for the fusion of the new layer by the heat of the flame.

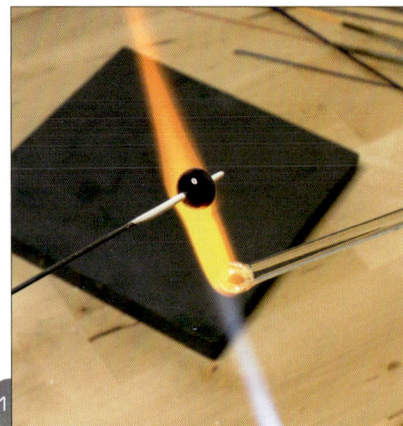

11/ Certain occasions allow for adding transparent glass to increase the depth of color and to obtain more volume.

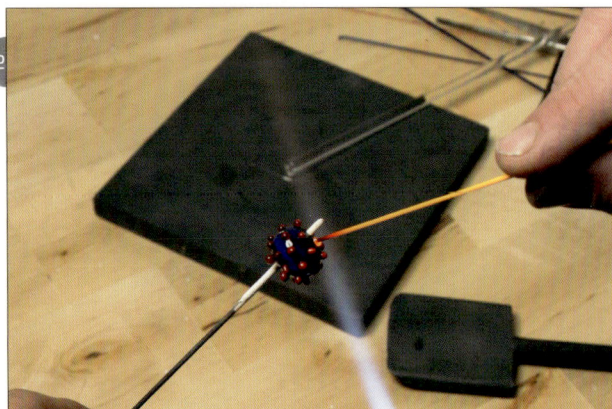

12/ Small amounts of glass from a thin rod can be applied to form grains of smaller size.

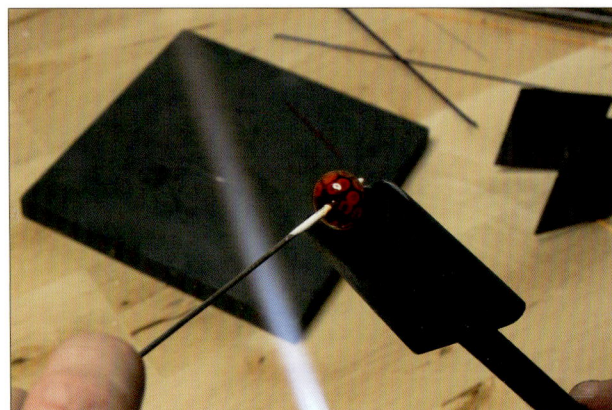

13/ This colored glass layer is partially fused to obtain small spheres of molten glass on the surface of the ball.

14/ The graphite spatula and other such tools can be used to shape the sphere, to flatten it, make it square or to stretch it, always while hot.

15/ The base can be used to flatten the bead as a cylinder and then to heat it again.

16/ Next, new glass strips can be added and then fused together.

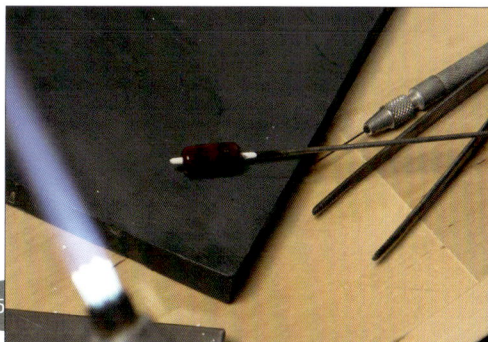

17/ Once the flame has been removed, leave the beads to slowly cool down on an isolating material such as thermite-vermiculite or a piece of thermal cloth. If the sphere is rather large, re-fire it at 500 degrees Celsius (930 degrees Fahrenheit).

Codinaorfebres. Necklace made from glass beads.

Embossing and Engraving

Embossing and engraving techniques allow for achieving volume with thin metal foil, as well as its decoration using various chisels and hammers. With proper use of these tools, the metal piece can be worked to its desired thickness on one of its faces while modeling the main face of the piece. The chisel is the most important tool; it is used to decorate the pieces or the cast elements to give them a particle surface hardness of the metal.

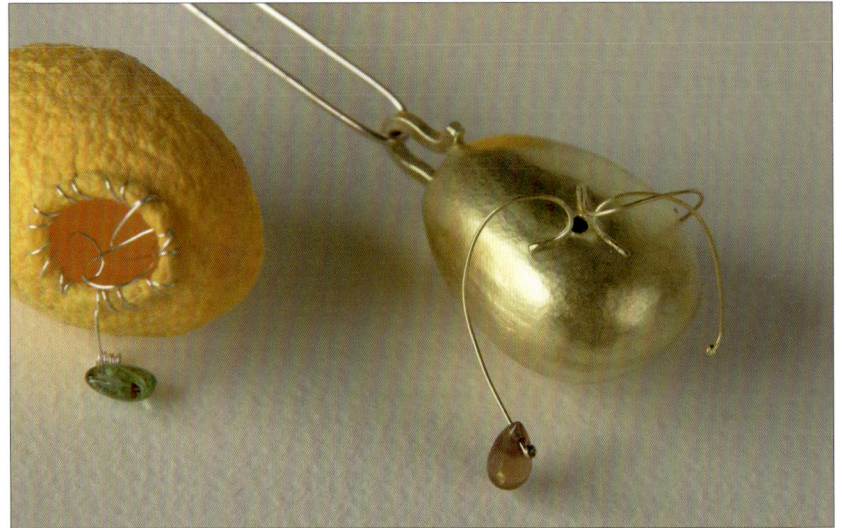

Walter Chen. Embossed gold piece, gold wire and tourmalines. The element is made of natural silk dyed with saffron and fixed with acrylic resin.

Embossing table with the basic tools used for engraving.

Carmen Amador. Bonjour, Monsieur Cézanne. Silver, gold, fine pearls, and synthetic ruby, 2009.

Set of punch chisels used for punching and giving volume to the sheet.

Tools

The essential tools for embossing and chiseling are various hammers with a particular design as well as three steel chisel types: modelers, tracers, and punches. Although they can be bought from a specialized retailer, chisels can also be made in a shop, giving them various shapes and textures to be able to make different decorations and textures.

Another necessary element is a support from a triangular piece of wood and a half sphere of iron; the latter contains the previously molten lead inside of it and is filled with a particular material to affix the metal plate. A wooden box can also be used, the important part is that it must be heavy so as not to move while chiseling.

Chiseling hammer with a wooden handle made from ash, which provides the required flexibility for performing good work.

A set of flat modeling chisels used for shaping and forming the volume once the sheet has been punched.

Set of tracer chisels with straight and curved shapes. They are used to initially draw the image as well as to work or to emphasize a new profile or outline onto the metal.

23

Making a Chisel

In order to make a chisel, select a steel rod of medium hardness and cut it into sections of ten or eleven centimeters (4 inches). The steel must be allowed to be reheated and tempered with either water or oil; if tempered with water, the steel becomes harder than when tempered with oil.

1/ Start with a piece of medium-hard steel rod, which can be of a variety of different profiles.

2/ To be able to shape the steel it must be heated at the tip to an intense red color. This way it becomes softer and allows for it to be forged.

3/ The steel is hammered vertically on the anvil to increase its width at the tip.

4/ The chisel is repeatedly heated and hammered, this time on its sides, until it is slightly broader.

5/ The chisel after repeated heating and forging.

6/ While cold and using a coarse file, work the chisel so as to give it the desired profile and definition. Next, polish with successive sheets of emery paper until the surface is very fine and allows for later polishing.

7/ The polishing process provides the steel surface with a perfect finish. The brilliance is entirely necessary, as each hit with the chisel transmits it to the silver.

Preparing the Pitch

In order to emboss and chisel the metal, the sheet or piece needs to be fixed to a mass with the right amount of elasticity. This allows for it to adapt to the concurring dilations of the metal while being embossed.

There are different formulas for pitch, depending on the climate and the work to be performed. Generally, it consists of a sticky and somewhat elastic element like colophony, a grease or oil component like olive oil, which gives the pitch its appropriate elasticity when added in the right proportion, as well as a very fine red earth, like ochre.

To prepare the pitch, 1 kg of colophony is slowly dissolved at low heat in a saucepan while gradually adding 2 kg of red ochre so as to avoid the formation of chunks. Add 100 cm^3 of olive oil or turpentine. If you want to soften the pitch, add more oil or turpentine.

Once the pitch has been prepared, pour it over a cold steel sheet and divide it into pieces, which are reheated inside a box or the chiseling bowl.

Three basic ingredients: colophony, red ochre, and olive oil.

Once the mixture is perfectly homogenous it is poured onto a cold sheet of iron to be broken into small pieces. It can also be poured directly into boxes or chiseling spheres.

TRADITIONAL TECHNIQUES

It consists of fixing a sheet of molten metal over the pitch by slightly heating the surface. To get a good adherence, slightly bend the metal sheet´s edges over the hot pitch so that no air remains between the two. Next, mark the desired design onto the metal with a steel pen and use different chisels and tracers to complete the design before punching or creating the first volumes.

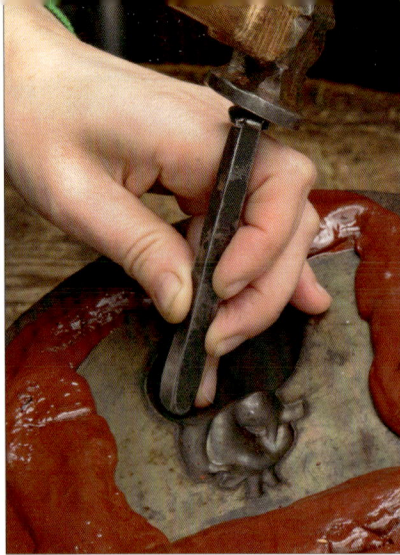

After tracing the volume, it is necessary to emboss the metal with force; hammer from the back side of the sheet with larger-sized punches and chisels.

The hit should be completely perpendicular over the punch or chisel so as to allow its smooth and even advance over the sheet, denting the surface on its path.

The chisel needs to be at a 90-degree angle to the hammer to result in a short and repetitive hit.

1/ Once the volume has been chiseled, the piece is extracted from the pitch, the metal is heated again and the volume is chiseled again on a bronze anvil. To extract the piece from the pitch, heat it with the blowtorch and pull at the sheet with pliers.

2/ To place it again onto the pitch, slightly heat the surface while the sheet is pressed against the hot pitch. Once cool, continue to chisel.

3/ Continue with ever finer chisels until the volume is perfectly defined.

ONCE
UPON A TIME
CHERNOBYL

4/ In order to judge the depth, place a piece of modeling paste inside.

5/ Once removed, the paste clearly shows the depth and quality of the work.

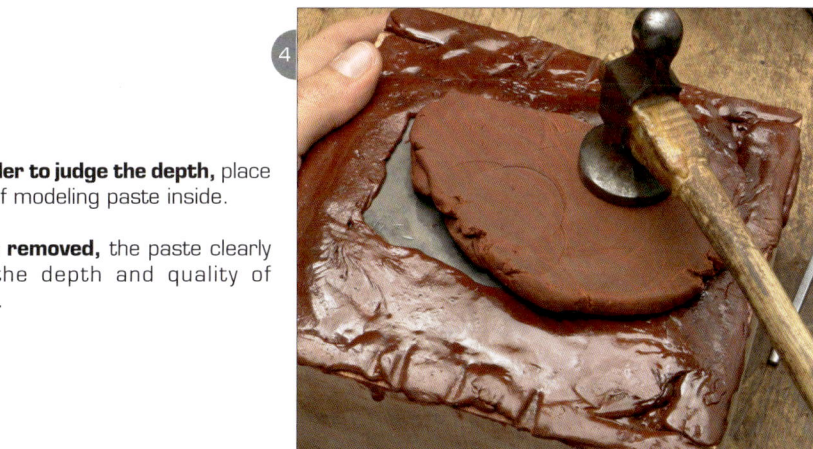

6/ During this process it is necessary to remove the sheet from the pitch to reheat it and to change its face to be able to shape the main face. Start by fracturing the pitch laterally with a small chisel.

7/ Once the pitch has been cracked at the edges, slightly heat with the torch and free the sheet from the pitch.

8/ Use the torch to burn off the rest of the pitch as well as to reheat the metal. Next, strip it in acid.

9/ After reheating the sheet, fill the volume with scraps of pitch that are heated with the torch until they melt.

10/ Reposition the sheet on the pitch and model it by using different flat modeling chisels of different sizes to obtain the final volume of the piece.

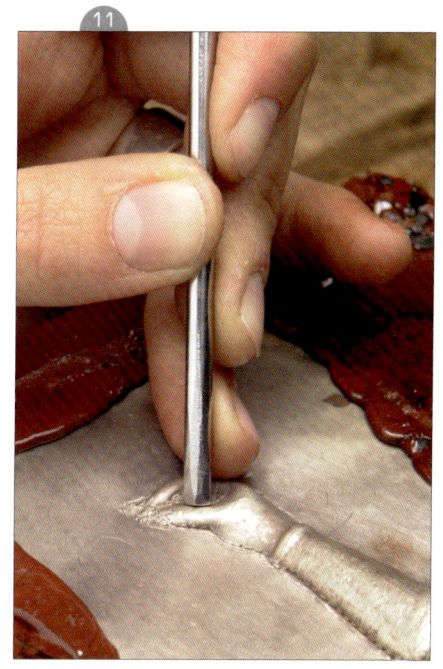

11/ Girding chisels allow to outline or to draw new lines onto the piece.

12/ Again the outline is flattened with precision utilizing a flat chisel or punch on the bronze anvil, just like before.

13/ Once the volume has been finalized with the punches and chisels, cut out the outline of the arm with a fret saw and file the base. Next, affix the piece of porcelain provisionally and begin to build the support structure.

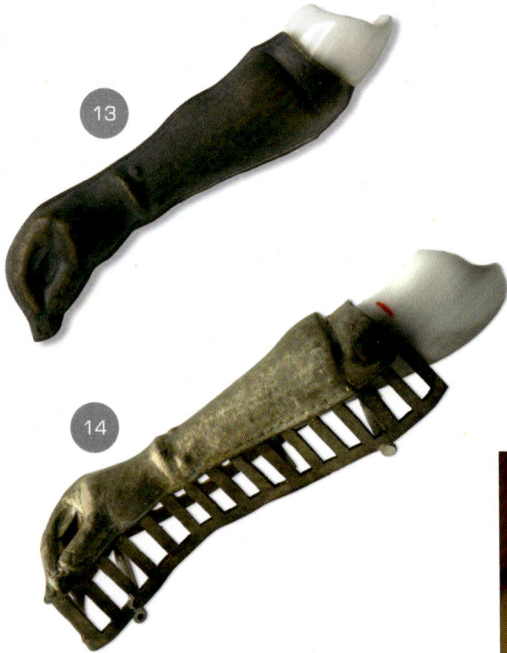

14/ The structure has been worked in alpaca, bending it and precisely adjusting it to the rim of the chiseled volume where it needs to be soldered. This structure serves the purpose of elevating the chiseled shape in order to solder the latch of the brooch to it.

15/ Once all the soldering has been done, the alpaca is oxidized. Use a tabletop blowtorch to heat it up a few times with the flame.

16/ The last thing to do is to add a piece of stainless steel wire, like that used in dentistry, to finish. Adjust the porcelain inside the structure.

17/ Detail of the finished closure and correct placement of the porcelain.

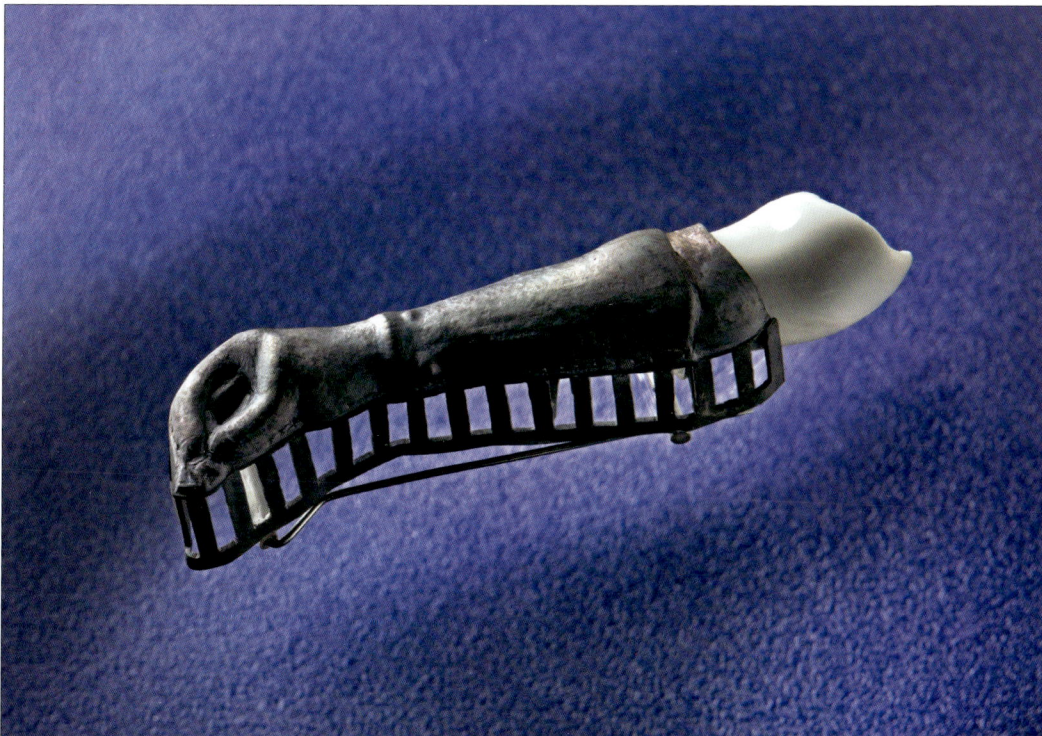

Carolina Martínez Linares. Alpaca brooch and porcelain, 2009.

Setting

Mounting gems on metal is considered a specialty within jewelry making, as the gems are an essential part of this craft. Nowadays, very precise mounts are done using microscopes, as well as other systems that employ sophisticated technology. In practice, it is important that the artisan understand how to perform a basic mount of a gem inside its frame, while it makes practical sense to perform the most basic mounts of a jewelry workshop in order to build new and original mounts from there.

Cordinaorfebres. Prototype and cast mounting in gold to fit an aquamarine.

Walter Chen. Brooch from natural silk dyed with saffron and fixed with acrylic resin, gold, ruby, stainless steel, and silver.

1/ Once the pitch has cooled, break it into pieces and heat them slightly with an alcohol burner to avoid burning.

2/ This way the pitch melts over the wooden shaft until it is thick enough to form the base for the mount.

Supports

Before starting work it is essential to anchor the metal mount on a rigid support. There is an ample selection of supports to which the piece can be affixed, however, the most common method to affix the mount is the use of a mixture of equal parts shellac, red ochre, and colophony, called mounting or setter´s pitch (which is more dry and less elastic than the pitch used for chiseling). These three elements are slowly melted for this pitch, and once the desired, uniform consistency has been achieved, it is poured onto a slightly moistened steel sheet. Leave to cool and break into small pieces, reheat until the homogenous mass allows the piece to be affixed.

3/ Carefully affix the mount on the top part of the shaft and put it into water to harden the pitch.

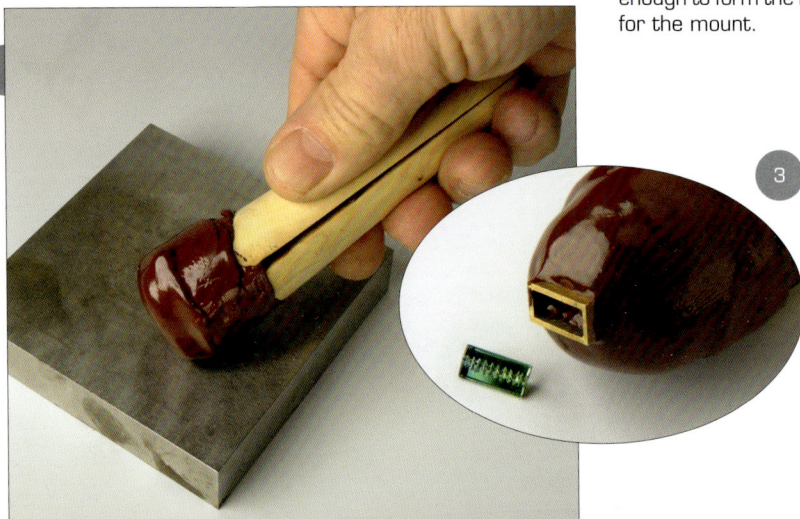

Burins
(Engraver's Chisel)

Burins are cutting tools with various different shapes made from very hard tempered steel. When they are adequately prepared, they allow adjustments to be made to the metal in order to set the gem inside the mount. It is also possible to decorate the metal and to perform precision work via cutting.

1/ Burins of different profiles and hardness are available. In order to work with them, a wooden grip has to be affixed to the burin first.

2/ In a grinder, a point is created on the reverse side, so that it may be easily inserted and fixed inside the wooden handle. Sometimes it is preferable to cut the burin with a sharp blow to get a smaller tool length.

3/ After the grip has been attached, the burin's shape and plane is cut, moistening the tip regularly to avoid overheating, as this will cause the burin to cut badly, or not at all.

4/ The metal from the tip is eliminated and the primary face of the burin receives an angled surface of about 45 degrees.

Common burin profiles: claw-shaped, flat, and half-round.

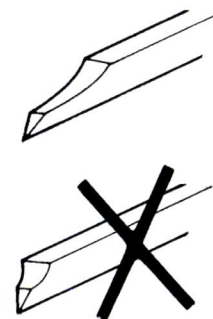

Correct burin profile.

Bezel Setting

This is a very common mount, which can have different shapes depending on the gem. Generally, the setting consists of a wire or sheet profile, which is thick enough to accommodate the profile of a gem and to work as a mount that adjusts to it perfectly.

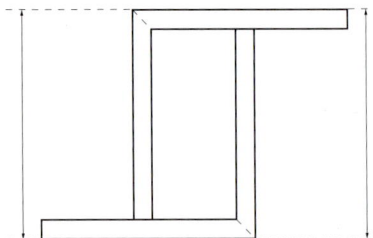

The metal must have a minimum thickness of 0.8 mm to crimp a stone of this kind. In order to create this frame, two pieces of metal are welded together in the form of "L" so that the gemstone is set to half the thickness of the metal.

1/ A spherical drill is used to eliminate the metal on the inside of the mount.

2/ Use a half-round burin followed by a flat burin to cut the metal to its proper angle and to achieve a proper set of the stone to the inner wall of the mount.

3/ It is important to remove the metal from the inner edges with the flat burin and to level and stabilize the gem.

4/ This stick is very handy to manipulate gems. It is made from a mixture of wood coal and beeswax, which is kneaded until its texture allows it to hold a gem by pressure, but without leaving wax on its surface.

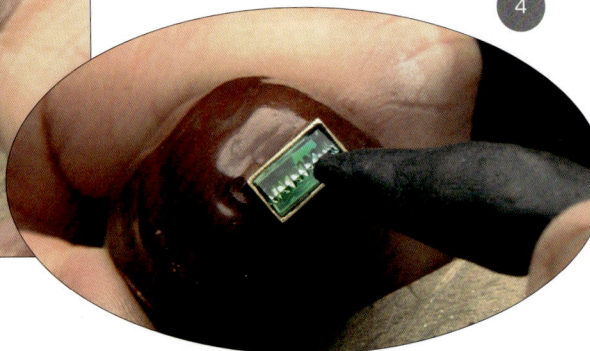

5/ Use a file to get rid of the metal on the outer side of the mount, which will result in the next phase being easier to perform.

6/ A pusher made from a piece of an old file handle is used to set the metal of the bezel over the gem.

7/ In order to set the metal over the gem, the direction of the applied pressure is varied continuously with successive movements so that the metal presses onto the gem.

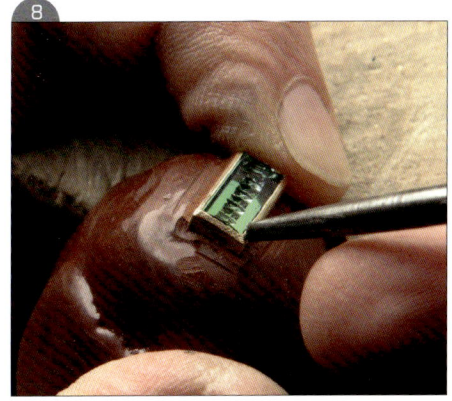

8/ A hammer is used to lightly push the metal previously deposited with the pusher, the objective being to flatten it perfectly and to adjust it to the gem while also hardening this area of the metal.

9/ A file is used to eliminate and to grind down the metal at an angle of about 45 degrees.

10/ Using a claw-shaped burin (V-shape), the irregularities in the area of contact between metal and gem are equalized.

11/ Emery paper provides the final shape to the mount.

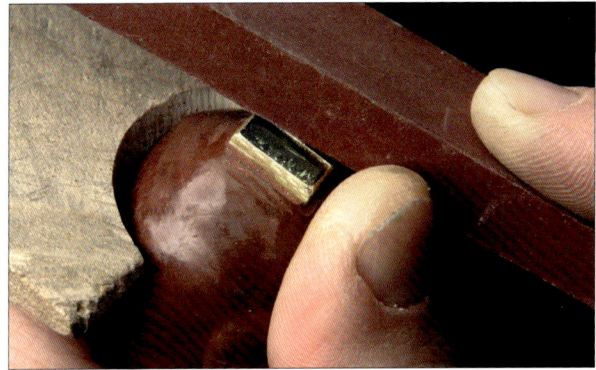

12/ Polishing is the final stage. It can be done directly with a polisher or, should the gem require it, using various types of desktop equipment to polish it and to give it that final shine.

10/ A thin burnisher is used to polish the metal that touches the gem.

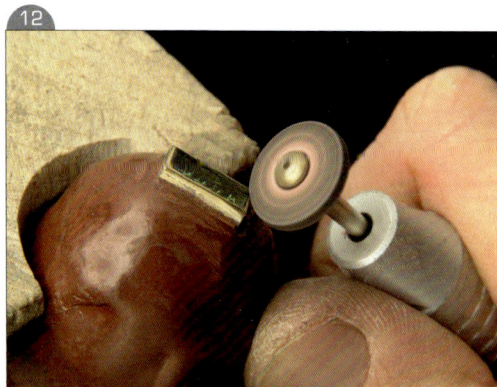

Diagramming mounting into the setting

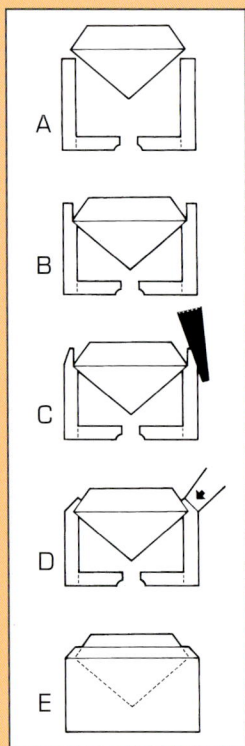

A. Based on half of the thickness of the setting wall, material is removed from inside the setting, with the aid of half round chisels.

B. Then the stone is properly mounted into the interior of the setting.

C. Once the stone is seated, use a file to remove some material from around the outside of the setting.

D. Close the setting's edge by pressing upwards or downwards here with the hammer, which closes the metal, giving the setting greater hardness.

E. Use a flat chisel to shape the interior of the setting where it is in contact with the stone. This will remove any imperfections. Then use a burnisher to give the interior of the setting a final gloss.

14/ The piece is removed from the setter's pitch and the handle by breaking both halves of the wooden handle, then boil the mount in water and ammonia to eliminate the pitch residues on the metal.

15/ Once the gem and mount are clean, the unit is polished.

Wire Prongs

Many mounts for gems are made from prongs of various profiles. This approach has the advantage of covering less of the gem since the metal is not continuous at its edges, as is the case with a bezel mount. There are many ways to make this kind of claw.

With any mount it is essential that the gem be perfectly adjusted to the interior of the mount.

1/ In this case, a structure was made from square wire, and different U-shaped prongs have been soldered to it that will hold the edges of the gem.

2/ The prongs are cut and filed at their lower end and a matching ring is soldered.

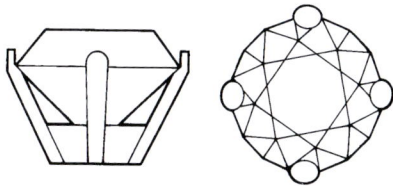

Adjustment of the prongs.

Codinaorfebres. Pendant featuring different gold wire profiles with olivine.

Mixed Mount Prototyped by Computer

The following mount is derived from a closed bezel where the metal of the bezels has been removed so that the gem is only supported by its vertex. The mounting procedure will be the traditional one.

Sometimes, the setting requires affixing mixed forms. This setting has been prototyped using a computer and molten gold.

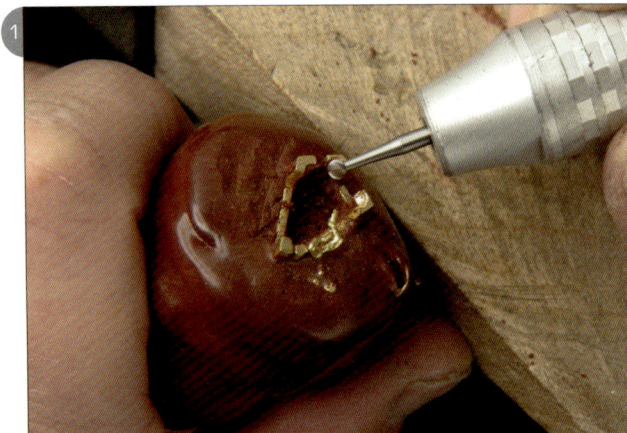

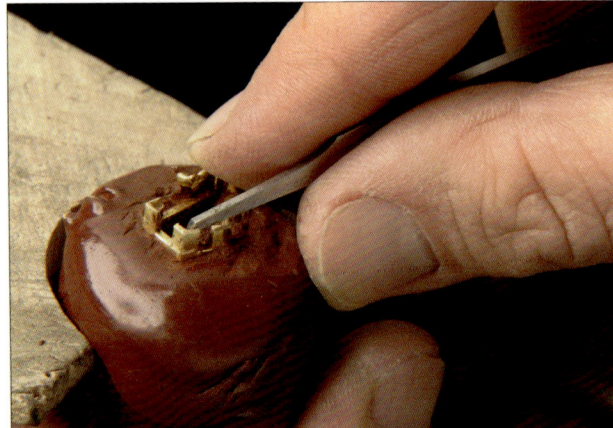

1/ First, the metal on the inside is lowered with various spherical drills to achieve a basic set for the butt end of the gem.

2/ Next, various burins are used to adjust the gem to the lower part of the mount so that it fits perfectly and is firm.

3/ With a file, the metal from the outer side is removed and shaped with the pusher and compressor hammer. Then, the file is filed to fit the outer part.

4/ Lightly polish with the claw-shaped burin and level the metal, which is in contact with the gem´s plane.

5/ Use a strong blow to break the support with the pitch and boil the piece in a little water with ammonia to completely eliminate the remains of the pitch.

Codinaorfebres. Yellow gold pendant with yellow beryllium.

Channel Setting

This technique is usually used to set several stones of the same size and shape in a line so that a continuous brilliance of the gem is achieved. This ring, made by Jona Aviñó, shows a variation.

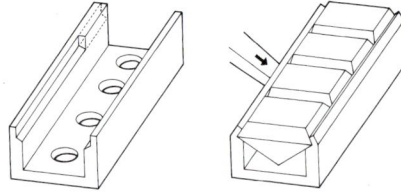

The traditional channel setting method introduces the gems from the top of the mount, and once they have been correctly set, the gem is mounted.

1/ This mount has been made by bending a solid sheet into a U-shape that matches the size of the selected garnet. It is soldered to the hollow structure of the ring made from a thin sheet of gold.

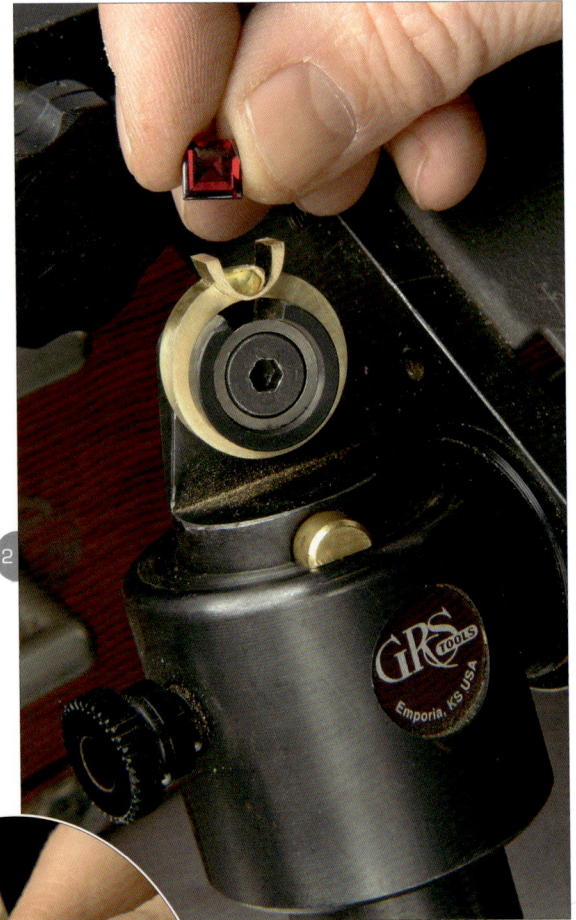

2/ Once it has been soldered, it is fixed in a clamp to be mounted.

3/ A flat burin is used to adjust the gem mount longitudinally; remove enough metal to place the stone inside the mount.

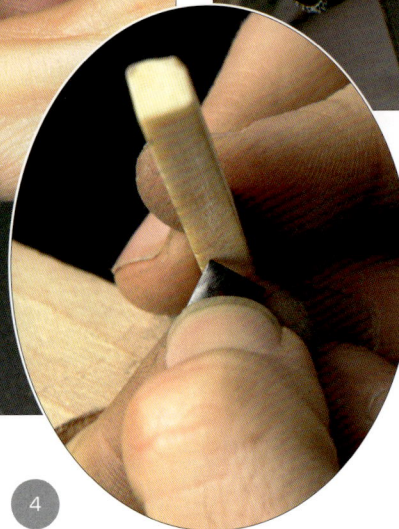

4/ Sometimes, the edge of the gem is too coarse for this type of mount, so it is usually finished with a lapidary stone before introducing it into the channel.

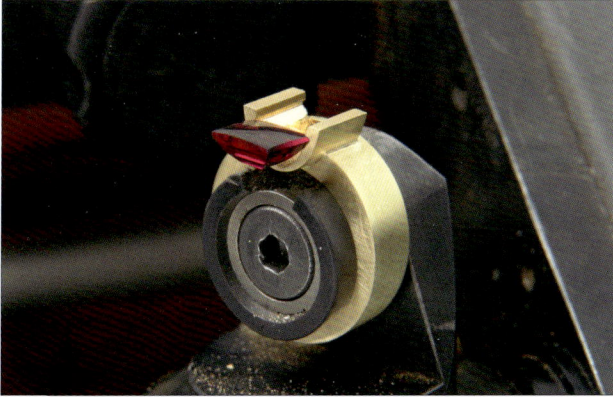

5/ A spherical drill and a flat burin are used to make a mount that perfectly fits the butt, or lower end, of the gem.

6/ Once the seat has been made, introduce the gem longitudinally into the channel without opening the metal from the top side. Another variation of this mount is to open the channel from above and introduce the gem into the channel this way.

7/ For the gem not to slide out laterally, a claw-shaped burin is used to make two grains at the end of each channel; metal from the end of the guide is lifted over the edge of the gem in the shape of a grain.

Joan Aviñó. Gold ring with garnet.

Image Transfer

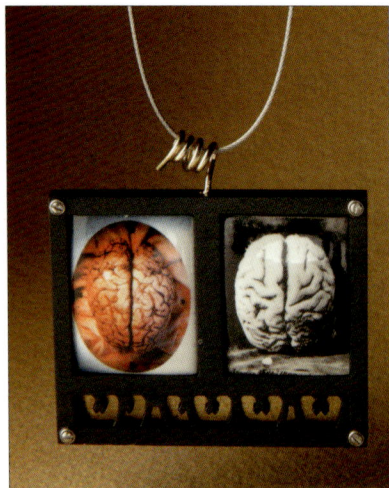

It is possible to transfer images onto metal or a variety of other materials using several methods. For example, images can be transferred onto moldable polymers from a photocopy, with its ink dissolved by a light solvent. Also, images can be placed onto porcelain with vitrifiable stickers, which are fired at high temperature, or sticky transfers by putting them onto the surface directly, or heating them. The procedures vary according to the desired effect and the surface that needs to be treated.

When using photocopies, it is important to raise the contrast and to use copy machines with toner, not laser copiers. Sometimes it may be helpful to apply a very light solvent to the photocopy, like eucalyptus oil, to help to dissolve the image.

Carles Codina. Silver pendant with color images applied to porcelain, 2007.

Alejandra Solar. Brooch.

Rings made by Alejandra Solar.

Alejandra Solar shows a building process where images are directly imprinted onto metal, including special colors for metal.

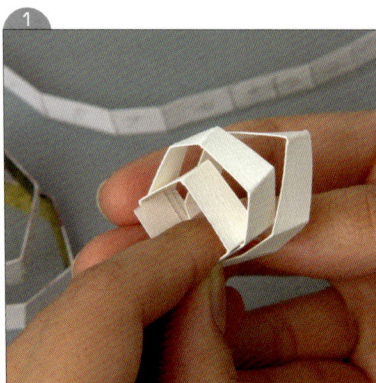

1/ First, a cardboard model is made to define the exact form of the project.

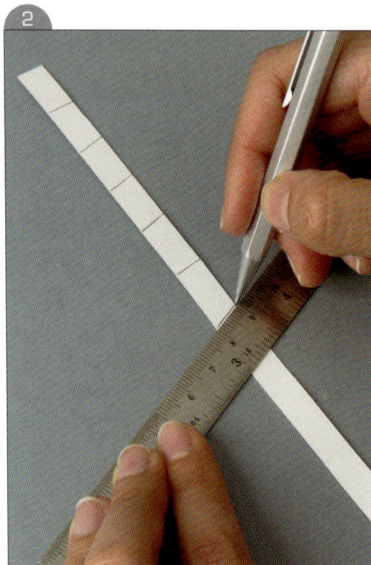

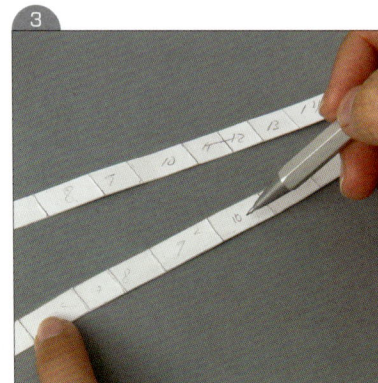

2/ Next, the bevels and posterior folds are marked.

3/ The sides that will give shape to the ring are marked.

4/ The identical pattern is marked onto a reheated sheet of alpaca, which must be perfectly smooth and polished.

5/ Using a metal tool, the piece is marked and slightly sawed at the bevels to facilitate the later introduction of the file.

6/ Deepen the bevel by cutting with a triangular file, which helps to achieve the posterior folding.

7/ The image has been imprinted on an acetate sheet. The intent was to provide a photocopy with abundant ink and a highly contrasted image.

43

8/ Select the area of the image to be transferred and degrease the metal before applying the image.

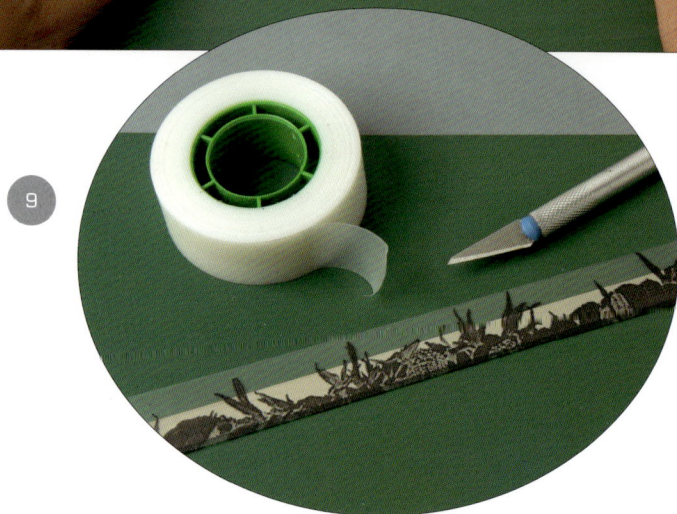

9/ The acetate is fixed with scotch tape to immobilize the image.

10/ Use a piece of kitchen paper towel between the acetate and an iron set for minimum heat, and press on the acetate sheet.

11/ Carefully remove the acetate and varnish the surface to protect the image.

12/ The back side of the ring has been painted with aerosolized paint. Previously, a metal base has been applied, followed by two layers of quality paint.

13/ Once dry, fold at the bevels. Use a pair of protected flat pliers to not damage the piece.

14/ This is how the author provides form to different ring or bracelet structures.

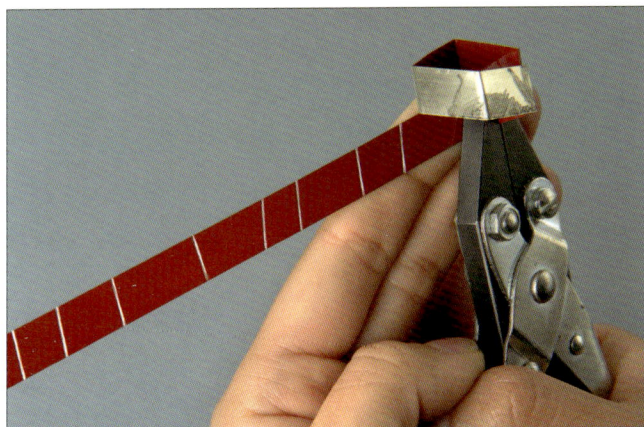

Alejandra Solar. Alpaca rings.

Alejandra Solar. Brooch.

Airbrush Painting

Klara Hedener. Silver brooch.

Alejandra Solar. Ring made from silver and machinable high density polymer (urethane), painted with spray paint. 2009.

Today's large variety of modern paints, which are offered through their manufacturers, allow metal to be covered with an infinite number of hues, with excellent properties for durability and color. It is a quick and effective way to provide color to practically any surface.

It is important to clean the surface to be treated, as well as to apply a thin base coat, quality paint, and a protective varnish. Several crisscrossing layers at the appropriate distance are applied, while adhering to the drying time indicated by the manufacturer.

1/ Machinable polyurethane is a noble and resistant material that can be easily worked. It is used as a base material to make molds that are to be copied via silicone molding, or which can be used directly as the original piece itself.

2/ This material is easy to drill, file, and polish, and once finished it is a rather resistant. Various grades of density and hardness are available, depending on the object to be made.

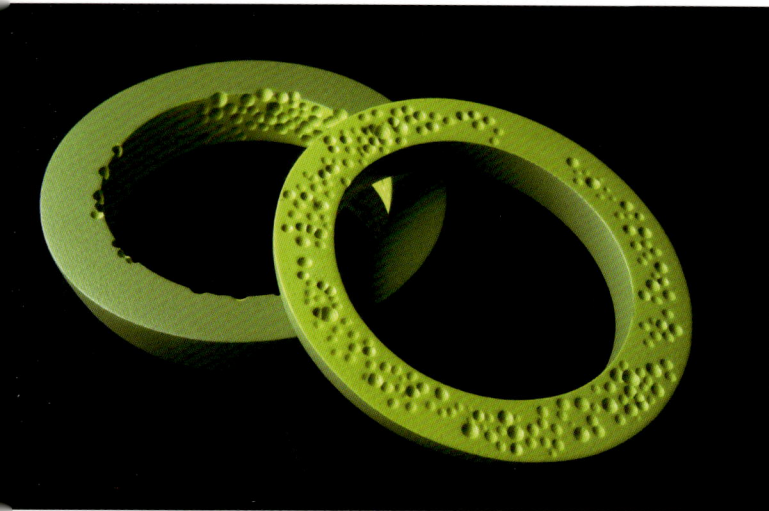

Marielle Debethune. Painted bracelet from machinable polymer.

3/ The surface is burnished progressively, with the last sheet of emery being a gauge 1,200. To further improve the quality of the finish, a very fine dishcloth or burnishing cloth is used.

4/ Once the surface has been thoroughly cleaned, an adequate primer is applied. In this case, as this is plastic material, a high quality synthetic primer is used. After drying, a second, very thin layer is applied.

5/ Two layers of paint are applied, with their directions being crossed. It is important to use high quality paint, if possible of the same brand as the primer. Leave to dry between each layer.

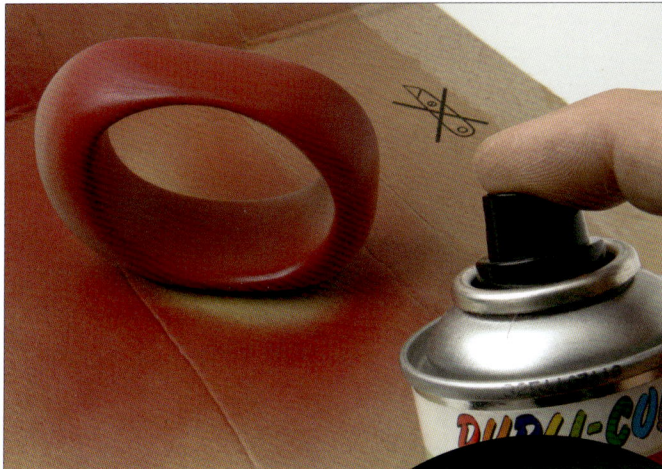

6/ Once dry, the piece can be left as is, or it can be protected with a layer of high quality epoxy varnish, applied from a spray can or with an airbrush. This varnish provides a slightly more brilliant tone to the piece and improves the hardness and resistance of the applied paint.

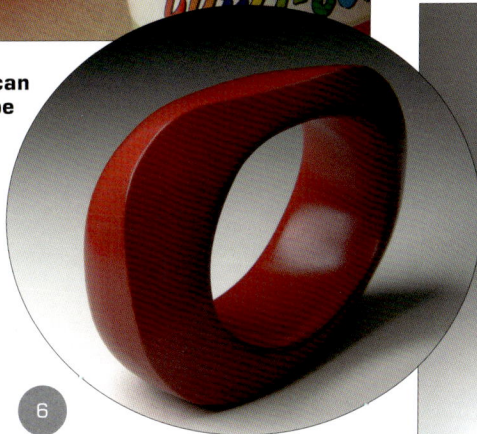

Carles Codina. Polyurethane bracelet.

Piece with Ivory Palm Nut, by Nicolás Estrada

The following example shows the making of a pendant in silver and ivory palm nut (tagua), a natural seed with a texture similar to ivory. Nicolás Estrada builds a small light receptacle with its own illumination from this nut, capable of shining light on ancient Native American myths of the many tribes who tried to explain the creation of the universe through the light of the sun and the moon.

1/ Once a palm nut has been selected for its smooth surface, the outer dark layer that covers it is removed until the desired pattern and texture is achieved.

2/ In order to hollow out the interior, several perforations are made with a coarse drill bit.

3/ A spherical drill is used to hollow out the inside of the palm nut until a uniform thickness of some 2–3 mm has been achieved. This makes it possible for light to shine through the thin wall.

4/ About a third of the upper section is removed. Next, a rim of about 2 mm is marked using a jewelry scribe.

5/ The entire rim of the palm nut is lowered to adjust the lid made from sterling silver.

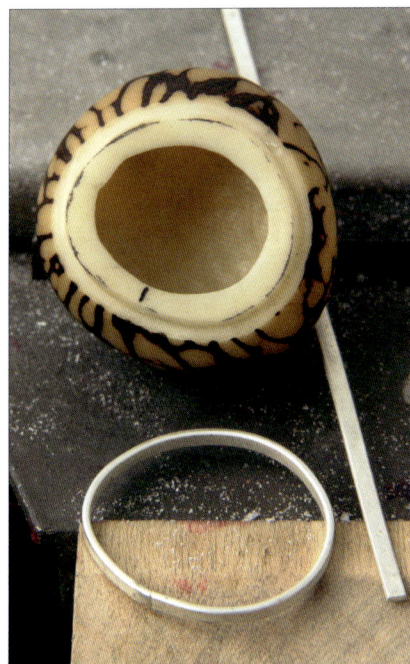

6/ A file is used to finish the details.

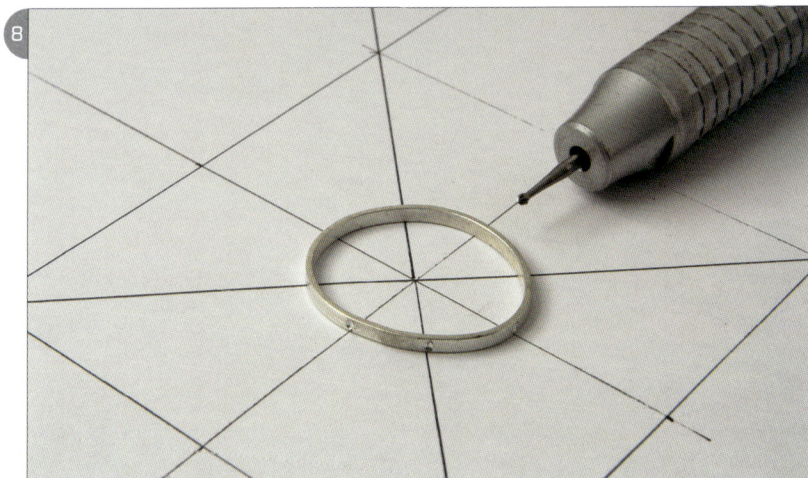

7/ A rectangular silver rim is drawn out and fitted to the rim of the nut using various pliers.

8/ Various perforations are marked and drilled at regular intervals onto the profile of the rim.

9/ The rectangular silver wire is soldered onto a sheet of 0.06 mm, then the extra metal is cut and filed.

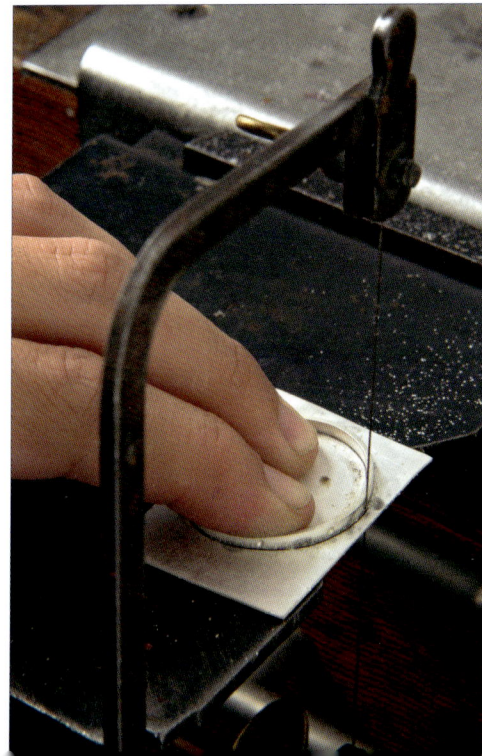

10/ Progressively level and polish the metal until a finely burnished surface has been achieved.

11/ The result should be a perfect fit of the silver lid on the palm nut.

12/ Two identical profiles are cut from a 0.06 mm sheet and are affixed to a wire with a rectangular profile to create a small volume. At the same time, the main structure has been shaped and two holes have been drilled.

13/ The idea is to place a small tube inside the smaller piece in order to allow for its movement once the piece is finished.

14/ A tube is soldered to the inside of the small structure before covering it with the second lid.

15/ It is covered with the second sheet and then soldered. Next, the unit is filed and polished until a uniform, smooth surface has been achieved.

16/ The palm nut is perforated with a very fine drill bit.

17/ Small silver wires are put into the resulting holes and the extra wire is cut off.

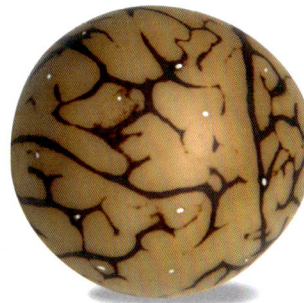

18/ The palm nut is polished again until the surface is nice and smooth.

19/ The metal lid is finished, with care taken to provide a good movement of the top structure.

20/ Once the two main elements of the piece are finished, the palm nut is adjusted to adapt perfectly to the metal structure.

21/ Image of the main body of the piece, leveled, before metal polishing.

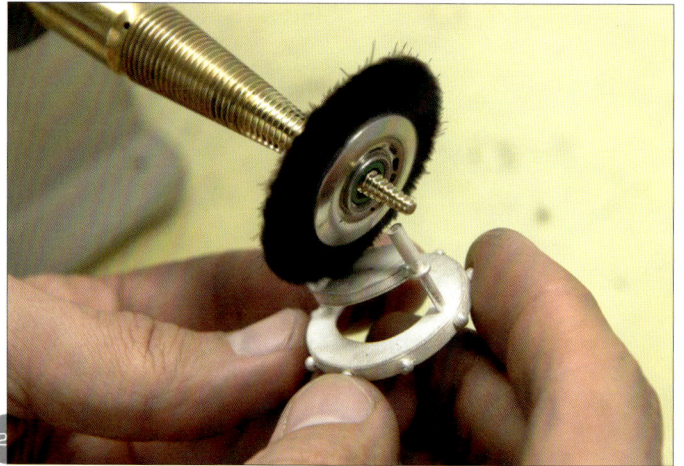

22/ It will be necessary to apply various phases of polishing until a perfect shine of the metal is achieved.

23/ The next step is to build the container for the batteries as well as the cord which will serve as the support for the pendant.

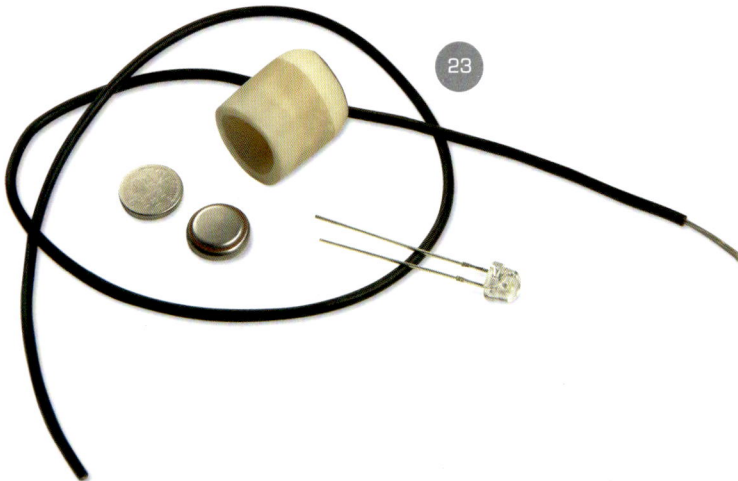

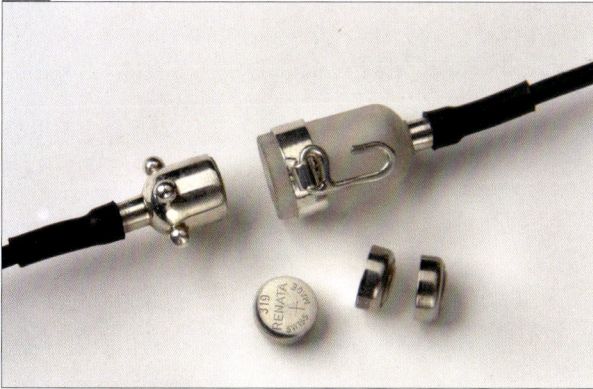

24/ A box for the photo-type batteries is built and the contact with the cable and the LED cell inside the palm nut is soldered.

25/ Finally, the palm nut is adjusted again and the final touches are given to the piece.

Nicolás Estrada. Pendant with silver and ivory palm nut, 2009.

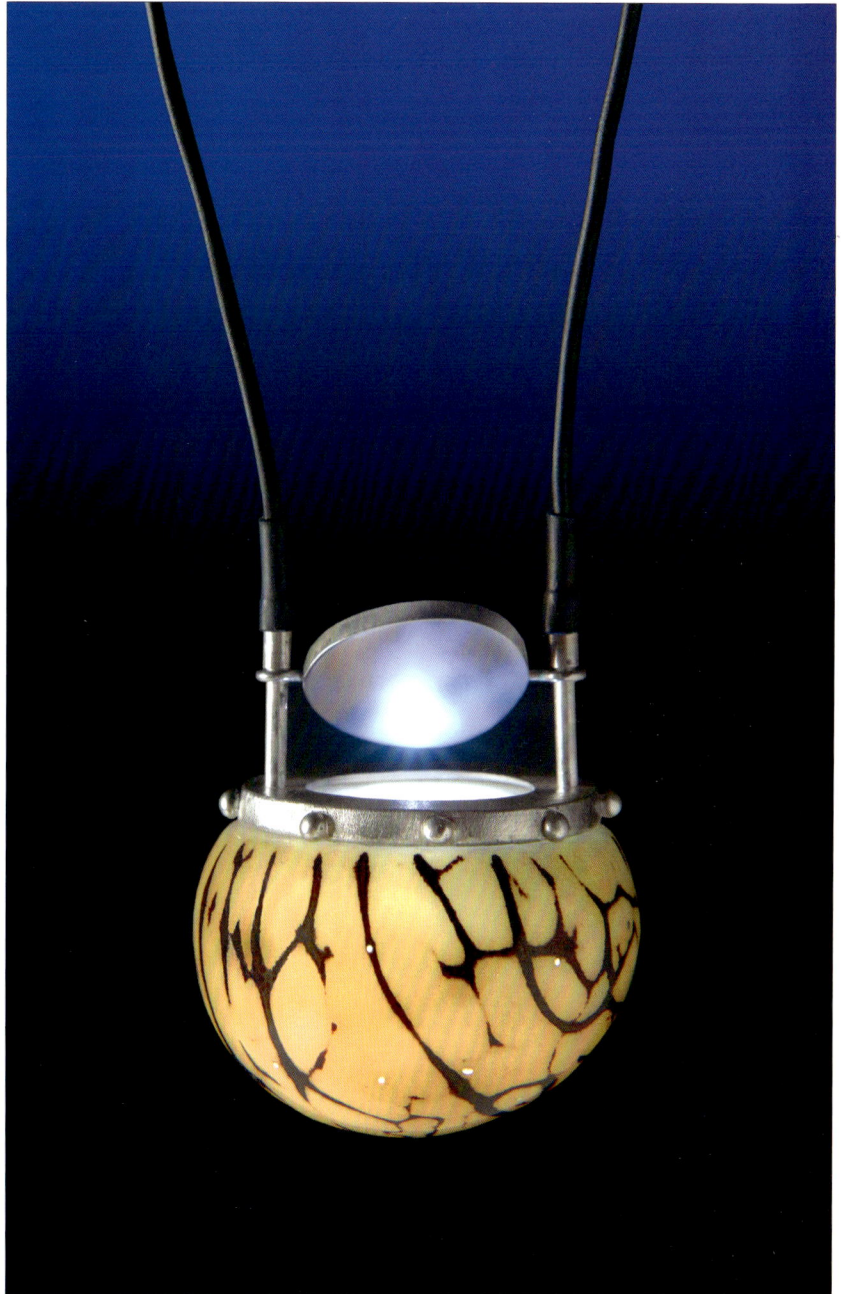

Gold Pendant with Tourmaline by Joan Aviñó

Gems are a noteworthy element of any piece of jewelry, and due to their value and natural beauty, they deserve to be emphasized with respect to the formal structure of the piece. This is why it is essential to create a perfect set and to conclude it with an adequate mount. After selecting various types of natural bark, the jewelry maker Joan Aviñó created a gold pendant by melting one of these pieces of bark in a microfusion cylinder.

During the creation, various processes are also displayed, such as the construction of a mount made from white gold for a tourmaline and its mounting. It also emphasizes the mounting of small diamonds directly onto the gold using a burin. Two methods of mounting, both of which are frequently used in jewelry making, are well worth knowing and developing.

1/ The main body of the pendant is created from the texture of a piece of tree bark. A mold is made from this piece and wax is injected into it. Once the wax is removed it will be filled with 18 ct. gold.

2/ Various pieces are created to select the one that is most appropriate for the project. The grooves are eliminated and the pieces are properly finished before building the various elements of the pendant.

3/ The chosen gem for this project is a green tourmaline of 1.82 ct. A rectangular white gold wire of 1 mm thickness has been laminated to form its mount.

4/ The metal is adjusted to the profile of the gem using pliers, making sure that the edge of the gem will sit exactly in the center of the width of the wire. Next, the edges are soldered.

5/ A piece of white gold wire of round profile is bent and soldered to the base of the gem's mount.

6/ The extra wire is cut away, inside as well as outside.

7/ Next, a sheet of 0.08 mm thickness is soldered to the base of the bezel and the extra exterior material is filed away.

8/ The entire exterior of the mount is polished with emery paper, first using coarse, then fine grain.

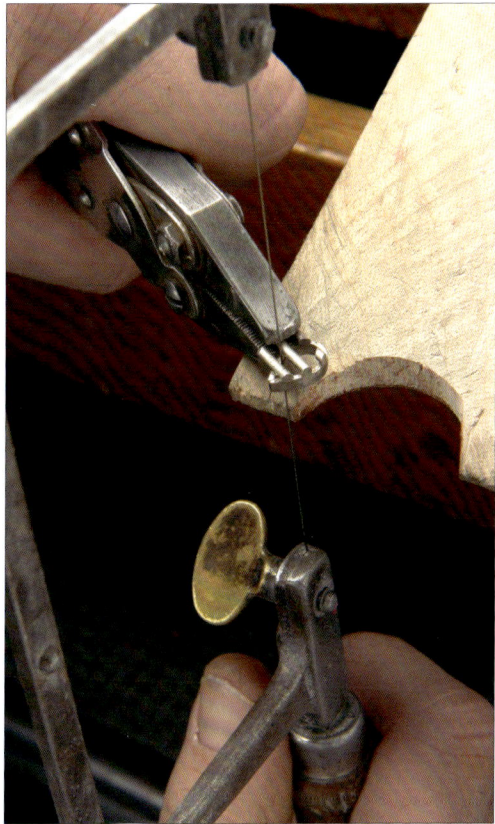

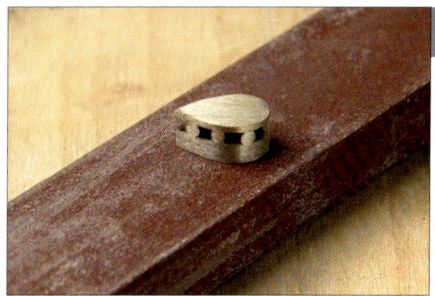

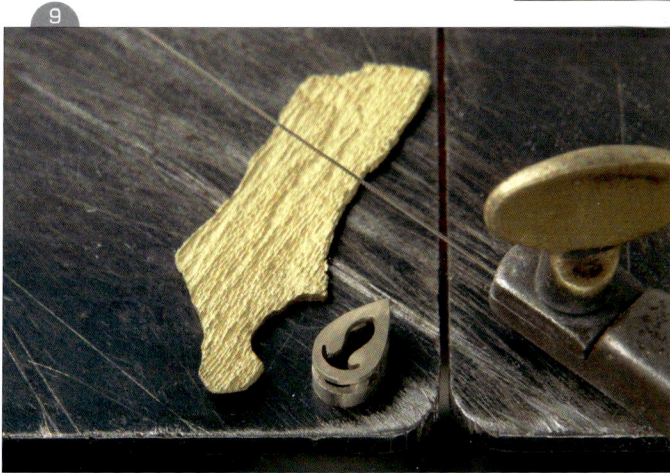

9/ A decorative cut is performed at the base of the mount, then the white gold mount is fitted to the yellow gold body.

10/ The two structures are soldered together, making sure that they adjust well to each other.

11/ A rectangular wire of 1 mm thickness is bent so as to adjust to the curve, which has previously been cut into the yellow gold piece. Both elements are soldered together.

12/ Once the diamonds for the decoration of the white gold piece have been chosen and classified, the piece is drilled vertically with a 0.05 mm bit.

13/ A spherical drill is used to widen the perforations so that the gems will fit better.

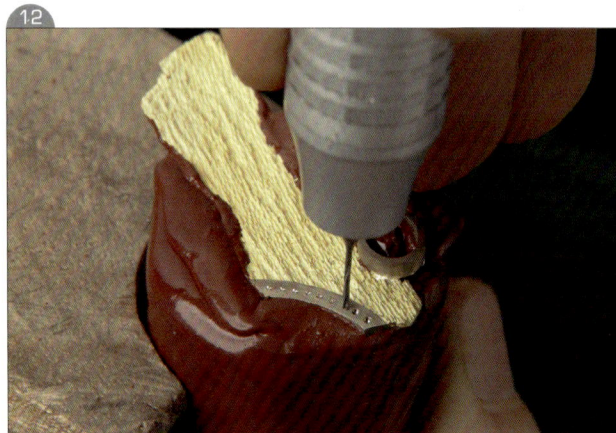

14/ Each diamond is fitted inside its seat and a claw burin is used to lift four grains over the gem to affix it.

15/ After profiling the metal, the grains are rounded using a tool with a concave tip, applying a rotary movement over each of the lifted metal grains.

16/ To set the tourmaline, various burins are used to cut the inside of the mount made of white gold so that the gem is perfectly adjusted inside the metal.

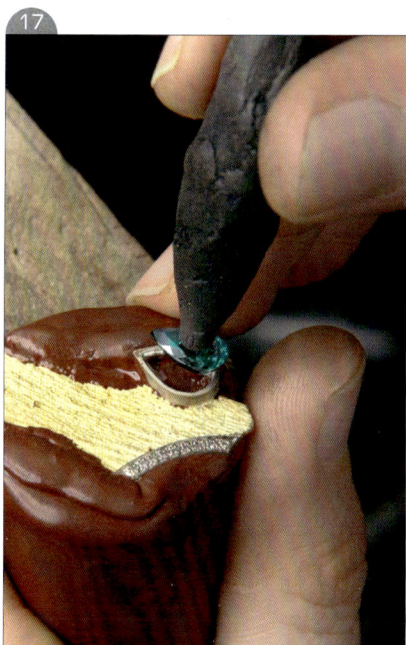

17/ The exterior metal is cut over the gem and profiled with different burins.

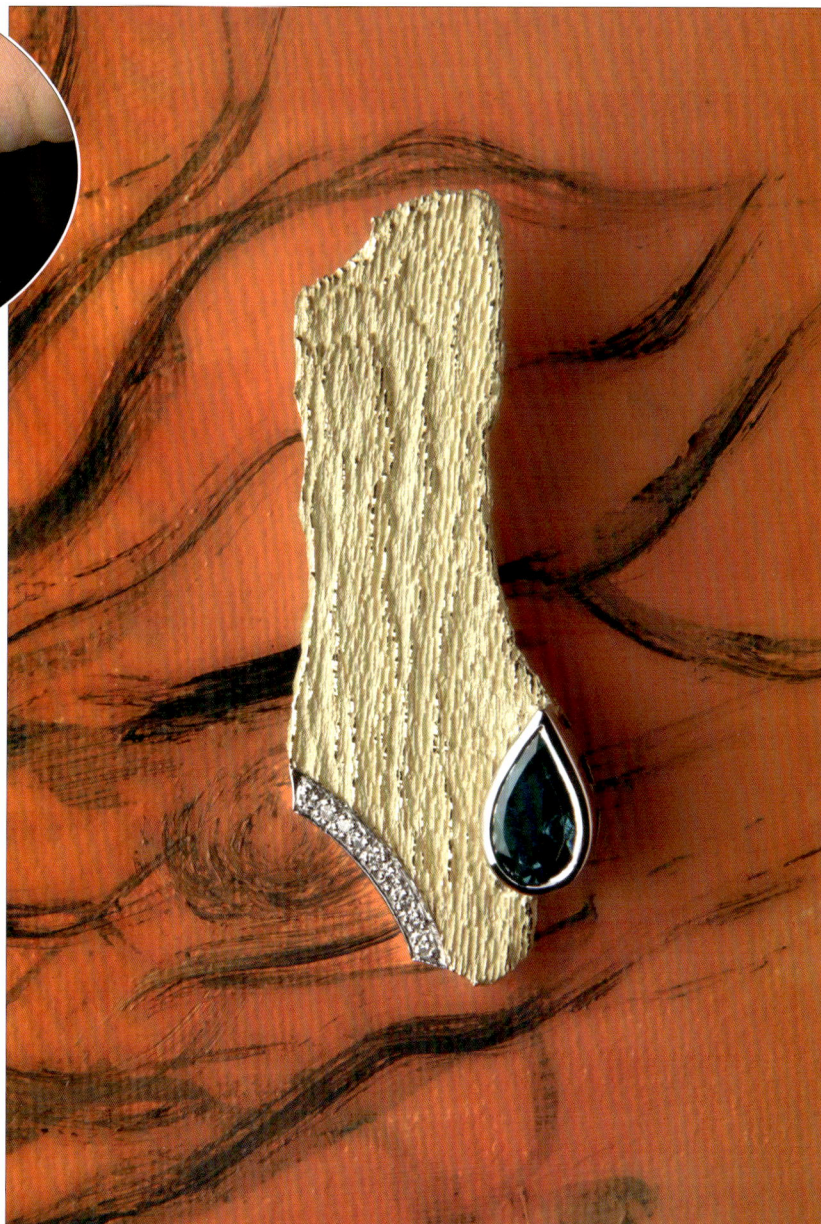

Joan Aviñó. Yellow gold pendant and tourmaline.

Brooches with Highly Resistant Paint, by Carles Codina

Highly resistant paint is usually used to give color to vehicle bodies and to objects requiring a high durability and resistance to wear. An airbrush is needed to correctly apply this paint, particularly to small pieces, and a deliberate step-by-step process involving working in layers is advisable. This process can be used with jewelry, as long as you choose high quality materials and apply them carefully in the order given here.

The following guide shows how to make various objects, starting out with the casting of some cactus leaves, which are then transformed into jewelry objects and airbrushed with paint.

1/ First, different parts of cactus plants are selected and cut with a scalpel, then they are reinforced with liquid wax to make them more rigid. Next, several layers of natural hair lacquer are applied until a thin fixation layer has been achieved.

2/ Once the elements have been prepared, a microfusion cylinder is set up following the usual techniques.

3/ For good reproduction results, the microfusion oven is over-heated to 800 or 850 degrees Celsius [1472 or 1562 degrees Fahrenheit] at the peak of firing, and the time of firing is also increased if the casing allows for it. The purpose is to completely burn the organic elements at a higher than usual temperature.

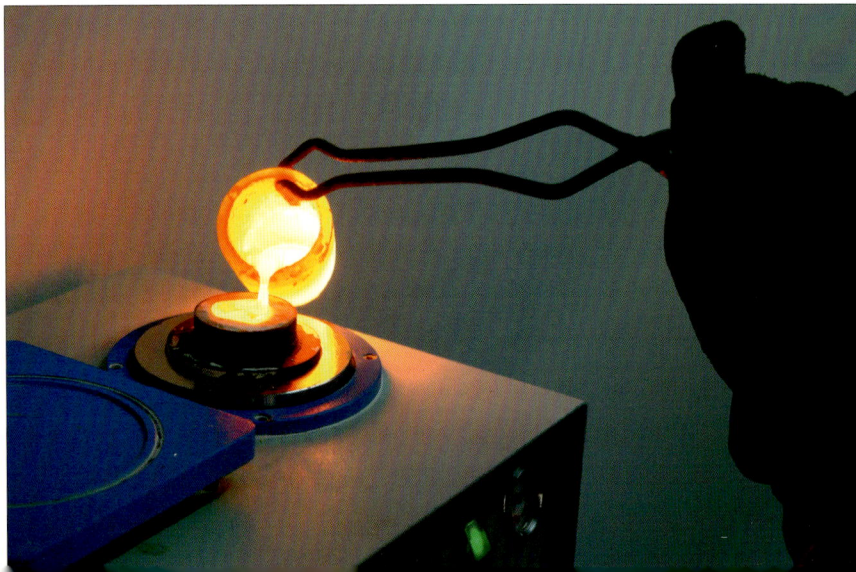

4/ The metal is poured into the cylinder, in this case, the leaves have been cast in a special silver alloy, but others such as bronze can be used as well.

5/ The pieces are cut and soldered according to the intended design.

6/ A special cutter intended to both press and cut different metal sheets is used for the body of the pieces. It consists of a piston housing a piece of urethane—a kind of flexible plastic.

7/ While hitting the piston inside a press, the urethane in its interior is deformed and penetrates into the steel cutter, shaping the metal towards the inside of the steel profile.

8/ The excess metal is cut away from each piece with a jigsaw and both sections of the piece are filed with a flat file to provide a perfect fit between both halves.

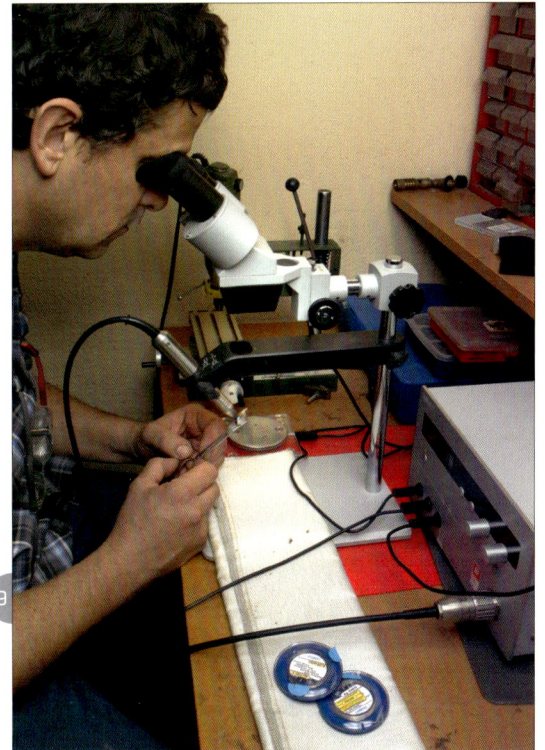

9/ Now is the time for soldering. Any traditional soldering method can be applied, or the two sections can be soldered with an arc welder.

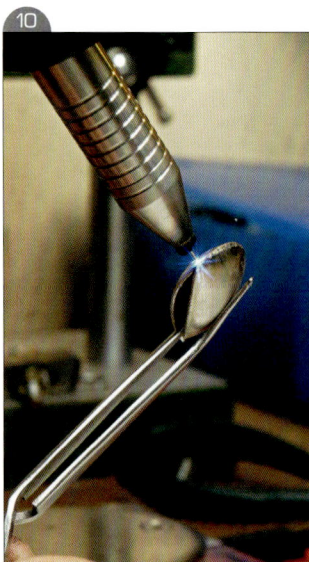

10/ The two halves are fused together without the need for soldering material.

11/ Once the fusion has been achieved, the extra material is filed away. Then, the metal surface is leveled and polished.

12/ Rings are soldered to the main body of the parts, depending on the design of the piece and its use.

13/ All the elements necessary for building the piece need to be soldered, including wires and hooks, in order to build the object.

14/ In order to apply successive layers of primer, color, and varnish, several supports are prepared. They will prevent the clean metal surface and the paint from coming into contact with fingers while painting, and will also allow the complete access to all the surfaces to be airbrushed. It is important to clean and degrease the piece thoroughly before applying any coating.

15/ The priming consists of applying various very thin layers of high-quality epoxy primer. The proportion used here is 80% epoxy primer, 20% epoxy catalyst, and 20% special epoxy solvent. Two crossing layers are applied and left to dry for five to ten minutes between layers.

16/ Color is applied using the airbrush with a size 5 tip. A small compressor pushes the dissolved paint via compression through a tip, while its intensity can be adjusted.

17/ High quality paint should be used. It is applied in very thin layers, leaving them to dry between applications. Matt black is dissolved with a specific catalyst and with a universal quality solvent.

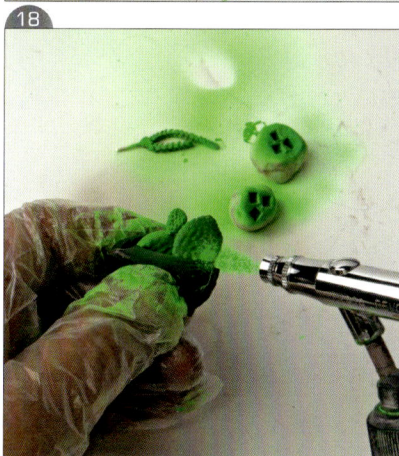

18/ In order to pass through the airbrush, the paint needs to be highly dissolved, usually two parts of paint and one part of quality solvent.

19/ Various layers are applied while changing direction, leave to dry for ten minutes between layers. Once the color applications are finished, leave to dry for at least half an hour before applying any varnish.

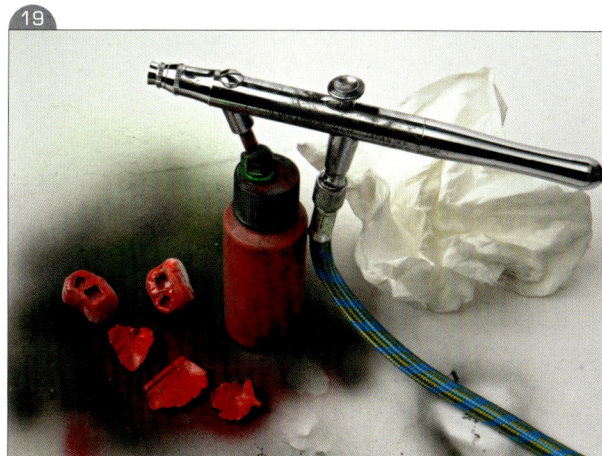

20/ The protective, brilliant varnish is mixed with a proportion of two parts of varnish, one part of the specific catalyst, and another part of acrylic solvent. Once completely dry, it can be burnished with a special polish.

21/ Here, the black paint has been left matt; however, a brilliant varnish can be applied to provide a shine to the piece and to make it more resistant. This auto body shop paint is highly resistant and can take scraping and knocks, which makes it perfectly suitable for the building of objects.

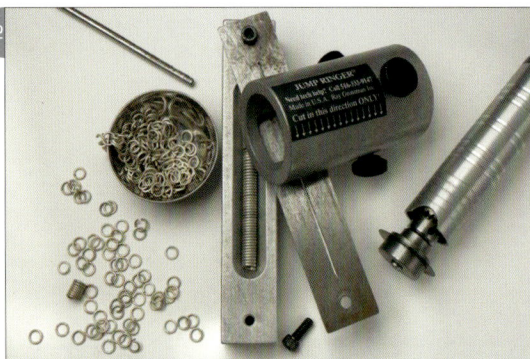

22/ In order to make a chain, a piece of 1 mm wire has been bent around a round, 6 mm rod. The idea is to make a wire spiral and then cut it with a cutter or with the arc saw.

23/ The pieces are united and form ever longer strands.

24/ The silver wire has been oxidized by submerging the finished chain in potassium sulfide, then it is fixed by applying heat.

25/ The final, finished piece.

Carles Codina.
Airbrushed brooch.

26/ The other pieces have been used to make various brooches. The clasps have been adjusted to their shape, glued, and screwed on with small watchmaker screws.

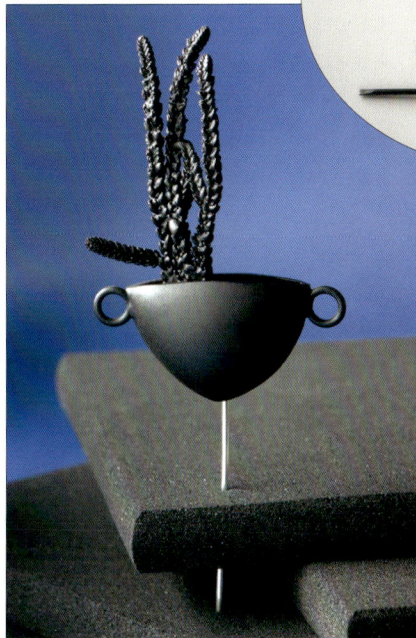

Carles Codina.
Lapel pin.

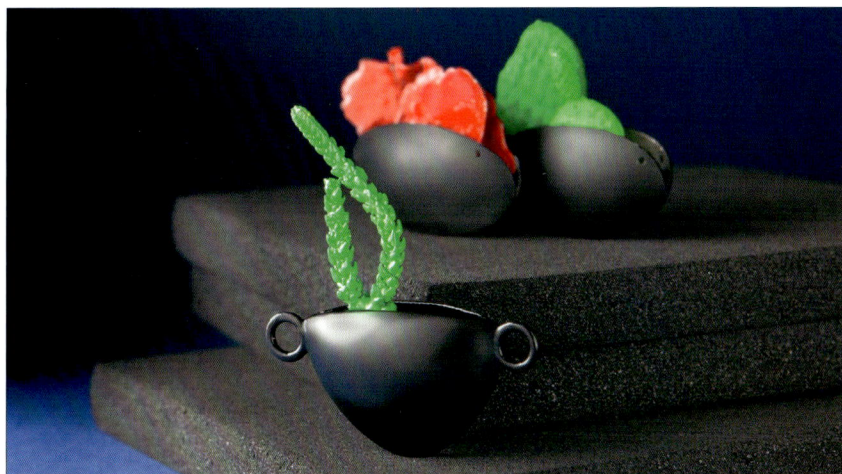

Carles Codina. Different painted brooches.

Acknowledgments

In order to be able to bring certain creative processes and various techniques to the broader public, numerous professionals have generously collaborated with their work. I am grateful to Joan Aviñó, Nicolás Estrada, and Alejandra Solar for their collaboration in various chapters of this book. Also, thanks go to Carolina Martínez and Nelly Van Oost for their collaboration with certain processes and techniques. I am also thankful for the generous collaboration of various authors who have contributed images of their work: Judy McCaig, Carolina Gimeno, Gaston Rois, Yoko Shimizu, and Elisabet Puig. My most heartfelt thanks goes to all of the authors who, for reasons of space, could not be included in the present volume.